JUSTICE FOR ALL?

The Rich and Poor in Supreme Court History 1790–1990

JUSTICE FOR ALL?

The Rich and Poor in Supreme Court History 1790–1990

Russell W. Galloway

CAROLINA ACADEMIC PRESS
Durham, North Carolina

ISBN:0-89089-421-3
LCC Number: 91-70323

Much of this volume was originally published as a limited edition under the title of *The Rich and the Poor in Supreme Court History*. In this present edition the text has been revised, updated, and expanded.

Contents

Preface

This edition brings the account of the rich and the poor in Supreme Court history up to date and up to the end of the Court's second century. When the first edition came out in 1982, the Burger Court had launched the Supreme Court's third conservative era (1969-present), and the prospects for the poor before the High Bench looked quite poor. After nearly another decade, the pattern is much the same. A dominant six-vote conservative bloc confronts a three-vote moderate-liberal coalition.

In fact, recent appointments have pushed the Court farther to the right. Warren E. Burger's 1986 retirement put William H. Rehnquist, the Court's most conservative member, in the Chief Justice slot and brought Antonin Scalia, a brilliant, energetic conservative, on to replace the aging Burger. The 1987 retirement of Lewis F. Powell, the Court's "man in the middle," and 1988 seating of Anthony M. Kennedy also moved the Court to the right. Last year's retirement of William J. Brennan and seating of David H. Souter reduced the liberal wing to one and probably added still another vote to the dominant conservative bloc.

The current Court is very conservative. The conservatives are activists as well. They proved that in 1989 by rewriting the nation's most important civil rights statutes and converting the equal protection clause into a constitutional barrier against government efforts to remedy discrimination against racial minorities.

Moreover, as in 1982, the prospect is for the Court to move still farther right. The two oldest Justices are Thurgood Marshall (82) and Harry A. Blackmun (82), the two most liberal Justices. The likelihood of a future Court without liberals is higher than ever.

So, as in 1982, the prospects for the poor in the Supreme Court are not bright. The poor and their advocates will have to seek other playing fields, especially Congress, if they wish to get federal government aid in their struggle against economic inequality.

Part One
The Court and the Constitution

1

The Supreme Court's Role in Economic Controversy

The United States Supreme Court opened for business in February 1790 pursuant to article III, section I, of the federal Constitution, which provides, "The judicial Power of the United States, shall be vested in one supreme Court, and in such inferior Courts as the Congress may from time to time ordain and establish." Justices are nominated by the President and must be confirmed by the Senate. Justices may serve as long as they wish "during good Behavior." Should misbehavior arise within their ranks, Justices may be removed from office only through impeachment proceedings conducted by the United States Congress. The number of Justices serving at any one time may be altered by statute. Over the years, the Court's size has fluctuated from six to ten members before settling in 1877 on the current number of nine.

Since its inception, the Supreme Court has had the authority to affirm or reverse many decisions made by state courts and lower federal courts. For approximately its first 135 years, exercise of this authority was legally mandated over a wide range of cases. But since 1925, the Court has enjoyed nearly complete discretion in selecting the cases it will hear. When evaluating requests for review of lower court actions, the Court is primarily concerned with questions of social or legal importance rather than questions of justice in individual cases.

On acceptance of a case for full review, attorneys representing both sides of the issue at bar attempt to persuade the Justices to rule in their favor. In the process, they present to the Court written briefs containing references to appropriate authorities, including relevant constitutional mandates, prior case decisions—that is, precedents—and statutory and administrative directives. In both briefs and subsequent oral arguments, the attorneys formulate an interpretation of the material cited, with each side hoping the Justices will endorse its viewpoint. Some while later, normally several months, the Court releases a written response that sets forth the majority opinion in the case and is accompanied by any concurring and dissenting opinions.

Given that the Supreme Court is constrained by such legal authority as the Constitution, statutes, and case law, one may wonder how the Justices' treatment of the rich and the poor has been able to vary sufficiently to warrant anything more than cursory attention. The central reality, however, is that interpretation is an enormously flexible process. The Justices, in fact, possess a great deal of freedom to write their personal preferences on an issue into any opinion. Moreover, they may set precedent aside and create new case law when they wish. Hence, the controlling factor in many cases brought before the Bench is simply the Justices' own perceptions of whatever outcome they consider best.[1]

When a vacancy appears on the United States Supreme Court, generally by reason of death or retirement, the attitudes of the President responsible for filling the empty seat become of paramount importance in the selection of the new Justice. It is not surprising, then, that the economic, political, and social philosophies held by a nominee play a major role in the appointment process. Throughout the country's history, Presidents have usually been acutely aware of the Court's great power to interpret the law. As a result, these Chief Executives have sought to appoint jurists whose policy views most closely accord with their own. In most instances, the Senate has approved these appointments quickly and methodically.

With the founding of the Republic, George Washington, for example, initiated the first conservative era of Supreme Court history by selecting conservative Federalists to fill all of the Bench's original six seats. Andrew Jackson later reversed that pattern and initiated the Court's first liberal era, lasting roughly from 1836 to 1890, by appointing Justices who shared the views of Jacksonian democracy. In the early 1920's, Warren Harding extended the Court's second conservative era, which lasted from 1890 to 1937, by choosing four conservative Justices. Franklin D. Roosevelt, in his turn, brought on the Court's second liberal era, 1937 to 1969, with his appointment of eight fellow New Dealers to the Court. Under Richard Nixon, the third conservative era commenced, an epoch that lasted through the Reagan administration and is likely to continue for many years beyond.

---

1. As William O. Douglas put it in his autobiography, "[Chief Justice Charles Evans] Hughes made a statement to me which at the time was shattering but which over the years turned out to be true: 'Justice Douglas, you must remember one thing. At the constitutional level where we work, ninety percent of any decision is emotional. The rational part of us supplies the reasons for supporting our predilections.' " W. Douglas, *The Court Years* (1980), 8. "In time I came to realize that Hughes was right when he said that a Justice's decisions were based 90 percent on emotion." *Id.*, 33.

From 1790 to the present, several images regarding the Court's attitudes toward the rich and the poor have emerged. Some commentators say the Court predominantly serves the corporate rich and typically decides cases in their favor. Others contend that the Court too often interferes with the political process on behalf of the poor, striving to protect the powerless from exploitation. Still others claim that the Court usually acts neutrally to balance competing interests and administer justice impartially. All parties agree, however, that the Court's duties include—because government's duties include—the responsibility to serve as a mediator of clashes between the haves and the have-nots.

From the best evidence of the past, the struggle between the rich and the poor has endured at least since the days when recorded history began. As American historian George Bancroft put it, "The feud between...the house of Have and the house of Want, is as old as social union, and can never be entirely quieted."[2] In the American 1700's, the rich-poor issue was so pervasive that many theorists consider it the most fundamental of all the Republic's early controversies. Clear recognition of the conflict's primacy can easily be traced back to the time of the Constitution's formulation.

A classic articulation of the rich-poor controversy was provided in Number 10 of *The Federalist*. There James Madison, principal author of the Constitution's Bill of Rights, the nation's fourth President, and a founding father, wrote:

> The most common and durable source of factions has been the various and unequal distribution of property. Those who hold and those who are without property have ever formed distinct interests in society. Those who are creditors, and those who are debtors, fall under a like discrimination. . . . The regulation of these various and interfering interests forms the principal task of modern legislation, and involves the spirit of party faction in the necessary and ordinary operations of the government.

Alexander Hamilton, the "prime minister" of the Washington administration and one of Madison's few intellectual equals among the founding fathers, agreed with his peer's contention and further asserted that the conflict between the wealthy and the needy should be a basic determinant of the very structure of government. According to Hamilton:

> All communities divide themselves into the few and the many. The first are the rich and well born, the other the mass of people. The voice of the

---

2. A. Schlesinger, *The Age of Jackson* (1945), frontispiece.

people has been said to be the voice of God; and however generally this maxim has been quoted and believed, it is not true in fact. The people are turbulent and changing; they seldom judge or determine right. Give therefore to the first class a distinct, permanent share in the government. They will check the unsteadiness of the second.[3]

America's second President, John Adams, whose understanding of political history and theory matched that of Madison and Hamilton, developed one of the most complete expositions of the rich-poor issue as it pertained to the nation's formative years.[4] From Adams' viewpoint, politics are founded directly upon economic interests. Society, he contended, is everywhere divided into two classes, a small group of rich persons and a large mass of poor. Further, he held, these classes are engaged in constant struggle, with the rich seeking to augment their possessions at the expense of the poor and the poor seeking to despoil the rich. The primary function of the government, then, is to mediate this struggle so that relative justice is done to all.

As a background to his commentaries on the Jeffersonian era, historian Charles Beard described Adams' economic and political thought this way:

> Adams' system of political science may be summed up in the following manner:
>
> 1. Society is divided into contending classes, of which the most important and striking are the gentlemen and the common people, or to speak in economic terms, the rich and the poor.
>
> 2. The passion for the acquisition of property or the augmentation of already acquired property is so great as to override considerations arising out of religious or moral sentiments.
>
> 3. Inevitably the rich will labor to increase their riches at the expense of the poor, and if unchecked, will probably on account of superior ingenuity and wisdom, absorb nearly all of the wealth of the country.
>
> 4. Out of the contest for economic goods arise great political contests in society, particularly between the rich and the poor. . . .
>
> 8. Therefore, the constitution must embody in it a representation of the rich and the poor as distinct orders; and a *tertium quid*[5] in the form

---

3. C. Beard, *An Economic Interpretation of the Constitution of the United States* (1913), 199 (hereafter cited as Beard, *Constitution*).

4. J. Adams, *A Defense of the Constitution of Government of the United States Against the Attack of M. Turgot in His Letter to Dr. Price* (1797). Adams' work has been discussed at length in C. Beard, *The Economic Origins of Jeffersonian Democracy* (1915), 299–321 (hereafter cited as Beard, *Jeffersonian Democracy*).

5. Some one thing acting as an intermediary between two other things.

of an independent executive holding for as long a term as possible should be introduced as a check on both the contending classes.[6]

Expression of this theme of class conflict based on inequalities of material wealth can be found in virtually all eras of American history up to the present. In Andrew Jackson's day, the dominant figure in the United States Senate, Thomas Hart Benton, stated in characteristically forceful language:

> There never has been but two parties . . . founded in the radical question, whether PEOPLE, or PROPERTY, shall govern? Democracy implies a government by the people. . . . Aristocracy implies a government by the rich. . . . [A]nd in these words are contained the sum of party distinctions.[7]

In the 1890's, Supreme Court Justice Henry B. Brown echoed the same sentiment.

> The history of civilized society is largely a story of strife between those who have and those who have not. . . . [Social conflict arises from] the desire of the rich to obtain the labor of the poor at the lowest possible terms, the desire of the poor to obtain the uttermost farthing from the rich. The cause and the result of it all is the unequal distribution of property.[8]

During the New Deal era, Robert H. Jackson, Franklin D. Roosevelt's attorney general and later a Supreme Court Justice, stated:

> Two kinds of power seem always in competition in our democracy: there is political power, which is the power of the voters, and there is economic power of property, which is the power of its owners.[9]

The list of concurring viewpoints on this subject among politicians, historians, and political theorists could be extended almost indefinitely.

As suggested, particularly by Benton and Jackson, the rich and the poor are viewed by many theorists not only as competing factions whose interests must be reconciled but also as the two basic sources of political power in a representative democracy. Generally, candidates must attempt to accumulate decisive power through an alliance either with the wealthy, whose money is needed for effective campaigning, or with the masses, who can directly supply votes in large numbers.

---

6. Beard, *Jeffersonian Democracy*, 316–17.
7. Schlesinger, *The Age of Jackson*, 125.
8. A. Paul, *Conservative Crisis and the Rule of Law* (1960), 85.
9. R. Jackson, *The Struggle for Judicial Supremacy* (1941), xii.

American political parties, despite their predisposition for playing both sides against the middle, have for the most part conformed to this theory, with conservative parties (the Federalists, Whigs, and post-Lincoln Republicans) siding with the rich and their liberal counterparts (the Jeffersonian Republicans, Jacksonian Democrats, and modern Democrats) affiliating with the poor.

In short, the political and economic tension between the rich and the poor accounts for what is widely regarded as the most fundamental of all political issues. Since, under the United States system of government, political controversies tend sooner or later to become judicial controversies, it is not surprising that this tension has repeatedly worked its way up to the Supreme Court in cases whose outcomes now form a major continuous thread of the institution's history.

After the fashion of political parties, Court Justices have to varying degrees identified with the aspirations of either the wealthy or the needy. Any understanding of the Court's role in the clash of the classes requires some delineation of the constellation of values, attitudes, and beliefs typically associated with the conservative and liberal viewpoints that have informed many Court opinions.

First, economic conservatism has typically been based on the conviction that governments should conserve the economic *status quo* and make no major attempts to redistribute wealth. Persons sympathetic with this outlook have classically contended that wealth is accessible to everyone who is willing to take advantage of natural opportunities. By this standard, the rich are fully entitled to savor the fruits of their superior abilities and effort, while poverty is seen as indicative of individual moral weakness.

To the economic conservative, the primary function of government in financial affairs should be to cultivate a favorable environment for the private pursuit of material wealth and to protect property owners against the recurring efforts of the poor to confiscate their holdings. At a minimum, government should refrain from redistributing property and from interfering with its accumulation and enjoyment. Economic conservatives have traditionally also tended to regard the Supreme Court, and the judiciary in general, as an important buffer against the dangers of uncontrolled democracy as reflected in the popularly elected legislative and executive branches of government.

Taken together, these attributes describe an ideal economic conservative type that no single Supreme Court Justice has ever fully and consistently embodied. However, over the course of 200 years, numerous individuals whose influence on the Supreme Court has been important have embraced these values at least in substantial part. Among the most noteworthy are Alexander Hamilton, Chief Justice John Marshall, Justice Joseph Story, Justice Stephen J. Field, President and Chief Justice William Howard Taft, Justice James C. McReynolds, President Richard M. Nixon, and President Ronald Reagan.

Economic liberalism, on the other hand, is characterized by a belief that the government should adjust the economic system so that wealth is distributed in such a way as to ease the burdens of poverty. Here, wealth is seen neither as a sign of superior moral worth nor as a valid basis for license to do as one will even to the detriment of the public good. Similarly, poverty is viewed as an unfortunate result of hereditary and environmental processes rather than as evidence of inferior character. To the economic liberal, government should protect the poor from exploitation and refrain from granting special privileges to the rich.

As with conservatives, no single individual has ever fully and consistently embodied all the qualities that comprise an ideal economic liberal type. But liberal values have often found favor with Presidents and jurists who have left their mark on Supreme Court history. Among their ranks are President Thomas Jefferson, President Andrew Jackson, Chief Justice Roger B. Taney, Justice Samual Freeman Miller, Justice Louis Dembitz Brandeis, President Franklin D. Roosevelt, Justice William O. Douglas, Chief Justice Earl Warren, and Justice William J. Brennan.

Caught up in ever shifting currents flowing between the opposing banks of economic conservatism and liberalism are political reform and counter-reform movements seeking to use legislatures and courts for the advantage of either the rich or the poor. After 200 years of fluctuating gains and losses on both sides, at least four themes have emerged out of these movements as recurrent in American history: 1) relief from excessive debts, 2) redistribution of wealth, 3) regulation of the behavior of the wealthy, and 4) support of organized action by the poor.

Regulatory laws have been enacted and social programs developed through the years to address each of these themes. Here are a few examples. For excessive debt: bankruptcy laws, stay laws (moratoria on debt foreclosure), and laws providing for currency inflation.[10] For redistribution of wealth: income tax, unemployment insurance, disabil-

---

10. Inflation of currency results in deflation of debts. As dollars become plentiful and less valuable, it becomes easier to pay debts.

ity compensation, old-age benefits, and other welfare programs. For regulation of the behavior of the wealthy: antitrust laws, minimum wage/maximum hour laws, child labor laws, laws prohibiting unfair business practices, laws regulating working conditions, and regulatory schemes based upon independent administrative agencies such as the Securities and Exchange Commission and the Interstate Commerce Commission. For organized action by the poor: laws supporting labor unions, boycotts, and class actions.

The history of the United States Supreme Court has unfolded against the background of such very practical matters as these.

2

The Constitution as an Economic Document

During the years immediately preceding the birth of the United States, significant political tensions characterized the relationship between the New World's rich and its poor. The traditional political climate in colonial North America had been aristocratic and based largely upon the disenfranchisement of persons who did not own substantial property. But, as the revolutionary period amply demonstrated, "democratic" sentiments concurrently enjoyed strong, widespread support.

The Revolutionary War brought about a shift in the existing power alignment between the haves and the have-nots. Many members of the propertied class were Tories who remained loyal to England throughout the conflict. When the revolution succeeded, Tories lost their political power and were supplanted by leaders who based their politics on direct appeals to the masses rather than on the protection of vested wealth. Progressive Era scholar Herbert Croly summarized these historical events as follows:

> The Revolutionary War, while not exclusively the work of the popular element of the community, had undoubtedly increased considerably its power and influence. A large proportion of the well-to-do colonial Americans had been active or passive Tories, and had either been ruined or politically disorganized by the Revolution. Their successful opponents reorganized the state governments in a radical democratic spirit. The power of the state was usually concentrated in the hands of a single assembly, to whom both the executive and the courts were subservient; and this method of organization was undoubtedly designed to give immediate and complete effect to the will of a popular majority.[1]

The post-war period from 1781 to 1789, when the Articles of Confederation were in effect, had a relatively populistic political climate. The federal government, at the time, lacked the power to tax and regulate commerce, and was therefore weak and ineffective. Real power lay in the hands of popularly elected state governments. These govern-

---

1. H. Croly, *The Promise of American Life* (1963), 31.

ments, responding to reform sentiments, enacted many statutes designed to help the poor. For example, bankruptcy statutes were passed
allowing debtors to discharge their debts without full payment. Other
legislative programs enacted to alleviate the burdens of the debtor class
included stay laws, paper currency statutes designed to produce inflation, and laws abolishing debtors' prisons.[2] Such statutes caused grave
alarm among the creditors whose claims they jeopardized.

The reform movement during the period immediately preceding the
Constitution had perhaps its most dramatic expression in Shays' Rebellion of 1786. A group of Massachusetts debtors led by Daniel Shays
sought relief from hard times through a variety of measures including
issuance of paper money to inflate the currency and reduce the weight
of their debts. When their efforts failed, Shays and his supporters engaged in armed revolt. Although the insurrection was quickly suppressed, it intensified the desire of the propertied class to create a government that would fully protect its interests.[3]

The convening of the 1787 Constitutional Convention in Philadelphia was the beginning of a counterrevolution in which the propertied
class sought to regain power and create a government designed in large
part to protect the vested interests of the rich against incursions by the
masses.[4] The "Conclusions" reached at the end of Charles Beard's *An
Economic Interpretation of the Constitution of the United States* vividly depict the attitudes of the creators and supporters of the Constitution with regard to the struggle between the rich and the poor.

> The movement for the Constitution of the United States was origi-
> nated and carried through principally by four groups of personalty [per-
> sonal property] interests which had been adversely affected under the
> Articles of Confederation: money, public securities, manufactures, and
> trade and shipping. . . .
>
> A large propertyless mass was, under the prevailing suffrage qualifi-
> cations, excluded at the outset from participation (through representa-
> tives) in the work of framing the Constitution.
>
> The members of the Philadelphia Convention which drafted the Con-
> stitution were, with a few exceptions, immediately, directly and person-
> ally interested in, and derived economic advantages from the establish-
> ment of the new system.
>
> The Constitution was essentially an economic document based upon
> the concept that the fundamental private rights of property are anterior
> to government and morally beyond the reach of popular majorities.

2. Beard, *Constitution*, 28, 31.
3. L. Pfeffer, *This Honorable Court* (1965), 35.
4. Beard, Constitution, *passim*.

The major portion of the members of the Convention are on record as recognizing the claim of property to a special and defensive position in the Constitution.[5]

As Madison explained on a number of occasions, the fundamental challenge facing the Constitutional Convention was to create a "democratic" government which would nevertheless provide full protection for the rights of the wealthy minority. This challenge was met by two different methods.

First, governmental power was so divided and fragmented as to make it extremely difficult for the majority to unite politically and impose its will on the minority. In this regard, a fundamental point to note is that the judicial branch was to be a keystone in preventing democratic majorities from imposing their will on the wealthy minority. "[T]he crowning counterweight to an 'interested and overbearing majority,' as Madison phrased it, was secured in the peculiar position assigned to the judiciary, and the use of the sanctity and mystery of the law, as a foil to democratic attacks."[6]

Second, limits were placed on the power of state legislatures to enact statutes encroaching on the interests of the rich. The most important of these limits were the prohibitions upon the emission of paper money and upon the enactment of laws impairing the obligations of contracts.[7] As Alexander Hamilton put it, "The too frequent intermeddlings of the state legislatures in relation to private contracts were extensively felt and seriously lamented; and a Constitution which promised a preventative was, by those who felt and thought in this manner, eagerly embraced."[8]

The conflict over the ratification of the Constitution was extremely intense and divided along class lines with the holders of property favoring and the debtor class opposing. As Beard stated:

> No one can pore for weeks over the letters, newspapers and pamphlets of the years 1781–1789 without coming to the conclusion that there was a deep-seated conflict between a popular party based on paper money and agrarian interest, and a conservative party centered in the towns and resting on financial, mercantile, and personal property interests generally.[9]

---

5. *Id.*, 324–25.
6. *Id.*, 161.
7. U.S. Const. art. I, sec. 10.
8. Letter from Alexander Hamilton to George Washington, May 29, 1779, quoted in Beard, *Constitution*, 180.
9. Beard, *Constitution*, 292.

The opposition to the Constitution almost uniformly came from the agricultural regions, and from the areas in which debtors had been formulating paper money and other depreciatory schemes.[10]

Charles Warren, author of *The Supreme Court in United States History*, the most influential account to date of the Court's history, reached conclusions almost identical to those of Beard on this point. Warren wrote:

Most of the opposition of the Anti-Federalists to the Constitution had been based on fears lest the proposed Federal Government should control the States in respect to their stay laws, their legal tender laws, their legislation as to British debts and loyalist properties and their State land grants and land titles.[11]

A typical opponent of ratification was Luther Martin, a member of the Constitutional Convention who later opposed ratification on the ground that the Constitution prohibited state legislation on behalf of debtor and agrarian interests. Martin's views on the contract clause illustrate this position.

There might be times of great calamities and distress, and of such extreme scarcity of specie, as should render it the duty of a government for the preservation of even the most valuable part of its citizens in some measure to interfere in their favor, by passing laws totally or partially stopping the courts of justice, or authorizing the debtor to pay by installments, or by delivering up his property to his creditors at a reasonable and honest valuation.[12]

As the foregoing shows, the debate over the Constitution, both during the drafting and during the ratification process, was essentially a debate between defenders of property and defenders of the propertyless in which the latter were resoundingly defeated.

It is perhaps fitting to conclude this discussion of the economic interests underlying the Constitution by quoting the conclusion (lengthy, but well worth careful attention) on this subject expounded by Chief Justice John Marshall in his *Life of George Washington*:

At length two great parties were formed in every state which were distinctly marked and which pursued distinct objects with systematic arrangement. The one struggled with unabated zeal for the exact observ-

10. *Id.*, 291.
11. 1 C. Warren, *The Supreme Court in United States History* (1922), 62–63 (hereafter cited as Warren, *The Supreme Court*).
12. Beard, *Constitution*, 205–06.

ance of public and private engagements. By those belonging to it, the faith of a nation or of a private man was deemed a sacred pledge, the violation of which was equally forbidden by the principles of moral justice and sound policy. The distresses of individuals were, they thought, to be alleviated only by industry and frugality, not by a relaxation of the laws or by a sacrifice of the rights of others. They were consequently the uniform friends of a regular administration of justice and a vigorous course of taxation which would enable the state to comply with its engagements. . . .

The other party marked out for themselves a more indulgent course. Viewing with extreme tenderness the case of the debtor, their efforts were unceasingly directed to his relief. To exact a faithful compliance with contracts was, in their opinion, a harsh measure which the people would not bear. They were uniformly in favor of relaxing the administration of justice, of affording facilities for the payment of debts, or of suspending their collection, and of remitting taxes. The same course of opinion led them to resist every attempt to transfer from their own hands into those of congress powers which by others were deemed essential to the preservation of the union. In many of these states, the party last mentioned constituted a decided majority of the people, and in all of them it was very powerful. The emission of paper money, the delay of legal proceedings, and the suspension of the collection of taxes were the fruits of their rule wherever they were completely predominant. . . .

Throughout the union, a contest between these parties was periodically revived; and the public mind was perpetually agitated with hopes and fears on subjects which essentially affected the fortunes of a considerable portion of society.[13]

The chapters that follow trace the fortunes of economic conservatives and liberals as they have brought their claims before the United States Supreme Court.

---

13. Quoted in *id.*, 297–99. This statement summarizes the main features of the eighteenth century variety of economic conservatism and liberalism.

Part Two
The First Conservative Era (1790–1835)

3

The Washington Court (1790–1800)[1]

During its first decade, the United States government was dominated by the Federalists, a political party composed primarily of the rich. As a leading scholar of the period put it, "Surely the frankest politicians who ever graced the American scene, the Federalists made no pretense of being other than what they were: upper-class Americans who had a natural born right to rule their inferiors in the social and economic scale."[2] George Washington, the nation's first President, was a loyal Federalist who selected his Federalist colleagues to fill essentially all the positions in the new government.

Although Washington was the nominal head of government, the dominant policy maker during the early 1790's was Alexander Hamilton, Washington's brilliant, energetic, and very conservative Secretary of the Treasury and author of the administration's major working papers. The intensely anti-democratic Hamilton distrusted the masses and devoted his main efforts to protecting and aggrandizing the interests of the propertied classes, especially the manufacturers, merchants, and financiers of the emerging capitalist system.

When Washington selected the six original members of the Supreme Court, he chose only Federalists who agreed generally with his and Hamilton's views regarding the purposes of the government. The original Court, which opened for business in February 1790, was composed therefore of property holders who shared the same anti-democratic bias that characterized the Federalist movement.

Consider, for example, the first Chief Justice of the United States, John Jay (1790–95).[3] The son of a wealthy merchant and husband of a

---

1. Useful accounts of this period include J. Goebel, *History of the Supreme Court of the United States: Antecedents and Beginnings to 1801* (1971); 1 Warren, *The Supreme Court* 31–169.

2. J. Miller, *The Federalist Era* (1960), 109.

3. When a Justice is introduced for the first time, his or her tenure on the Court will be indicated in parentheses.

member of the aristocratic Livingston family, Jay was a prominent lawyer who saw "the wise and the good" as locked in a never-ending struggle against the "wicked and the weak."[4] "[H]e was withal a conservative whose philosophy was succinctly expressed in the aphorism that
'those who own the country ought to govern it....' "[5] "[H]is entire
career and his character made him anathema to the lower classes and
their anti-Federalist leaders."[6]

The career of Justice James Wilson (1790–98) also vividly illustrates
the economic conservatism of the Supreme Court in its earliest years.
Wilson—"the Professor," as he was called at the time—was the "most
democratic-minded" of the Court's charter members.[7] He was a successful Pennsylvania attorney, a leading member of the Constitutional
Convention, and the co-author of the final draft of the Constitution.
Although perhaps the least conservative of the original Justices, Wilson
was the author of the contract clause, which provides, "No State shall
... pass any ... Law impairing the Obligation of Contracts."[8] The contract clause was the chief bastion of propertied interests during the Supreme Court's first conservative era. Wilson was heavily involved in
land speculation and has been described as a "member and legal protector of the creditor class."[9] Obviously, this Court, whose left wing
was occupied by James Wilson, was a very conservative Court indeed.

The remaining four original Justices were kindred spirits to Jay. John
Rutledge (1790–91) had formerly served as South Carolina's governor.
While holding that office, he had vetoed a proposed state constitution,
on the ground that it was too democratic. He then resigned when the
document was adopted over his veto.[10] William Cushing (1790–1810),
the only Justice to wear the traditional British judicial wig, presided
over a number of Shays' Rebellion trials and there earned the rebels'
hatred. John Blair (1790–96) was an independently wealthy Virginia
attorney and Washington's personal friend. James Iredell (1790–99)

---

4. Pfeffer, *This Honorable Court*, 37.
5. Miller, *The Federalist Era*, 32.
6. Pfeffer, *This Honorable Court*, 36.
7. *Id.*, 39.
8. U.S. Const. art. I, sec. 10. "[T]hat clause had been adopted for the express purpose of preventing the occurrence of the evils produced by the State stay-laws between
1783 and 1787." 1 Warren, *The Supreme Court*, 355.
9. Pfeffer, *This Honorable Court*, 39. Wilson's schemes collapsed and he spent his
final years on the run from his creditors.
10. Beard describes Rutledge as "one of the most ardent champions of the rights of
property in the [Constitutional] Convention." Beard, *Constitution*, 213.

was a Federalist leader from North Carolina and one of the most ardent supporters of the Constitution from that State.[11]

These, then, were the first Supreme Court justices. ... All were members or representatives of the propertied, creditor classes, and all believed that the purpose of government was to protect the rights of property against the covetous depredations of the lower classes.[12]

Table 1 shows the line-up of Justices on the original Supreme Court.

TABLE 1

Alignment of Justices, 1790

Left	Center	Right
	Wilson	Jay
		Rutledge
		Cushing
		Blair
		Iredell

For the remainder of the country's pre-Jeffersonian period (1790–1800), appointments to the Court did not appreciably alter the Bench's conservative character.[13] If anything, they probably moved the Court even further to the right. Rutledge's replacement, William Paterson (1793–1806), was a staunch Federalist and member of the wealthy Van Rensselaer family. Blair's successor, Samuel Chase (1796–1811), was "by far the most hated of the Federalist judges."[14] Chase's attitude on the rich-poor issue is strikingly illustrated by his famous Baltimore grand jury charge:

[T]he bulk of mankind are governed by their passions and not by reason. ... The establishment of universal suffrage will take away all security for property and personal liberty ... and our constitution will sink into a mobocracy, the worst of all popular governments.[15]

Oliver Ellsworth (1796–99), who replaced John Jay as Chief Justice after Alexander Hamilton declined the post, was a wealthy right wing

---

11. Iredell was not a charter member of the Court. Washington first appointed Robert H. Harrison, but Harrison resigned after five days and Iredell was appointed to replace him.

12. Pfeffer, *This Honorable Court*, 41.

13. Appointments not mentioned in the text include Thomas Johnson (1792–93) and Alfred Moore (1800–04).

14. Pfeffer, *This Honorable Court*, 86.

15. 1 Warren, *The Supreme Court*, 277.

Federalist. As Beard stated, "No member of the [Constitutional] Convention distrusted anything savoring of 'levelling democracy' more than Oliver Ellsworth."[16]

Bushrod Washington (1799–1829), who filled the chair vacated by the more moderate Wilson, was President Washington's nephew. Over the years, Justice Washington provided a virtual proxy vote for Chief Justice John Marshall (1801–35), who later transformed the Federalist credo of economic conservatism from a political platform into a set of legal principles that dominated the American legal system for decades.

As two early rulings illustrate, the Washington Court wasted little time before reading its principles of economic conservatism into constitutional law. In 1791, Rhode Island passed a statute granting a debtor a three year extension on the payment of his debts and exempting him from arrest and attachment during that period. Chief Justice Jay and Justice Cushing, on circuit, held the Rhode Island statute unconstitutional. Invoking Justice Wilson's contract clause, they wrote, "[T]he Legislature of a State have no right to make a law to exempt an individual from arrests and his estate from attachments for his private debts, for any term of time, it being clearly a law impairing the obligation of contracts, and therefore contrary to the Constitution of the United States."[17]

A few years later, the Washington Court, sitting *en banc* rather than on circuit, handed down *Ware v. Hilton.*[18] British debts were causing intense political excitement at the time. In Virginia alone, it has been estimated, Americans owed British creditors more than $2,000,000. Various States enacted laws rescinding these debts or allowing payment in depreciated currency. When the matter came before the Supreme Court, the Justices held that the state laws were contrary to applicable treaty provisions and that the British debts must be paid in full. This was in accord with the Federalists' economically conservative party line requiring strict enforcement of debts.[19]

The Supreme Court did not, however, play a major role in thwarting economic reform during the 1790's. In its first decade, the judiciary

---

16. Beard, *Constitution*, 196.

17. Champion v. Casey (unreported), discussed in 1 Warren, *The Supreme Court*, 66–68.

18. 3 U.S. (3 Dall.) 199 (1796), discussed in 1 Warren, *The Supreme Court*, 144–46.

19. Conversely, as Patrick Henry put it in a letter to George Washington, "The debtors are associated with the Anti-Federalists...." 1 Warren, *The Supreme Court*, 144.

was a very weak branch of government.[20] The Court had almost no business during its first five years, since time was needed for cases to work their way up through the new federal court system. The Justices spent most of their days riding circuit. When they did sit together, they functioned more as an admiralty court than as a third major branch of government.[21]

The Court's early weakness also stemmed in part from the Constitution's failure to define judicial power explicitly. The Court had to build its authority gradually. Not until 1819 did the Court attempt to exercise real political power in opposition to other branches of the federal government.

---

20. When John Jay declined reappointment as Chief Justice in 1800, he wrote, "I left the Bench perfectly convinced that under a system so defective, it would not obtain the energy, weight and dignity which are essential to its affording due support to the National Government, nor acquire the public confidence and respect which, as the last resort of the justice of the nation, it should possess." *Id.*, 173.

21. The Constitution confers jurisdiction on the Supreme Court to hear "all Cases of admiralty and maritime jurisdiction." U.S. Const. art. III, sec. 2. During the Court's first years many of the cases that managed to reach the Court involved admiralty jurisdiction.

4

The Court in Jefferson's Shadow (1801–1812)[1]

1801 was a milestone in Supreme Court history, because it marked the arrival of the "Great Chief Justice," John Marshall (1801–35). If a vote were taken among lawyers and judges to choose the most important person in the history of the American judiciary, Marshall would no doubt win by a large margin. More than any other individual, he laid the foundation of the American legal system, a foundation that still stands in large part today. Modest, sloppy in appearance, woefully lacking in formal legal education, uncommonly genial, Marshall proved irresistibly persuasive to most of his colleagues on the Court he dominated for a third of a century. "The last Federalist," he pursued the values of nationalism and economic conservatism with dogged consistency and astonishing success.

Ironically, 1801 also marked the inauguration of Marshall's cousin and most formidable antagonist, President Thomas Jefferson, who cast a shadow across Supreme Court history that eclipsed Marshall's light for at least a decade. Jefferson, the "man of the people,"[2] had a nearly lifelong hatred for Marshall and the aristocratic values for which Marshall stood.[3]

Jefferson proved to be the only adversary, with the possible exception of Andrew Jackson, who could hold Marshall at bay. The period of Su-

---

1. Helpful sources for this period include Beard, *Jeffersonian Democracy*, and 1 Warren, *The Supreme Court*, 170–399.

2. "As has been well said, 'Jefferson was a democrat, a people's man upon conviction. . . .' " 1 Warren, *The Supreme Court*, 321.

3. Jefferson was also aware of Marshall's mental powers. "Judge Story reported Jefferson as saying: 'When conversing with Marshall, I never admit anything. So sure as you admit any position to be good, no matter how remote from the conclusion he seeks to establish, you are gone. So great is his sophistry you must never give him an affirmative answer or you will be forced to grant his conclusion. Why, if he were to ask me if it were daylight or not, I'd reply, 'Sir, I don't know, I can't tell.' " *Id.*, 182. Later Jefferson wrote, "The Judge's inveteracy is profound, and his mind of that gloomy malignity which will never let him forego the opportunity of satiating it on a victim." *Id.*, 402.

preme Court history from 1801 to roughly 1812 can perhaps best be understood in terms of the struggle between Marshall's Federalist majority on the Court and Jefferson's anti-Federalist forces in the executive and legislative branches, a struggle in which Jefferson, for the most part, prevailed.

While conservative Federalists dominated the Supreme Court's first decade, concurrently, in another arena, their honeymoon was ending. In the early 1790's, Jefferson broke ranks with the conservatives who, under Hamilton's leadership, dominated the Washington administration and converted the federal government into something of a special preserve of Federalist property owners. After resigning from his position as Washington's Secretary of State, Jefferson began to gather the political support of voters who felt the national government should cease its practice of granting special favors to industrial and mercantile interests. According to Beard, "Hamilton's economic policies were the fundamental source of the party cleavage."[4]

> Thousands of small farmers and debtors and laboring mechanics were opposed to his [Hamilton's] policies, but they did not have the organization or consciousness of identity of interests which was necessary to give them weight in the councils of the new government. They were partly disenfranchised under the existing laws, and they had no leaders worthy of mention. . . . It required the astute leadership of Jefferson, and the creation of a federal machine under his direction, to consolidate the heterogeneous petty interests against the Federalist group.[5]

When Hamilton refused to make adequate concessions to the burgeoning democratic sentiments of the 1790's, even the Federalists split into a conservative wing under Hamilton's leadership and a moderate wing led by John Adams. The anti-Federalists' growing strength was vividly demonstrated by the presidential election of 1796, in which the moderate Federalist Adams eked out a razor-thin three-vote victory over Jefferson in the electoral college.

The anti-Federalist movement came to a head in the 1800 election, in which Jefferson defeated Adams. The significance of this election has been described as follows: "The Presidential election of 1800 marks a turning point in our national history no less important than does the adoption of our present Constitution. It signalized the initial victory of the first political party which professed to represent the American people."[6]

---

4. Beard, *Jeffersonian Democracy*, 112.
5. Beard, *Constitution*, 103.
6. Statement of Professor O. G. Libby, quoted in Beard, *Jeffersonian Democracy*,

The intense, almost apocalyptic anxiety felt by many wealthy merchants and industrialists regarding Jefferson's election shows that economic issues were what was fundamentally at stake in the contest. As "Decius" wrote in the Columbian Centinal, "Tremble then in case of Jefferson's election, all ye holders of public lands, for your ruin is at hand."[7]

What was it about Jefferson's political and economic views that seemed so revolutionary and dangerous to the leaders of finance and industry? One way to answer this question is to summarize the views of the intellectual godfather of Jeffersonian democracy, John Taylor, the Virginia farmer and political theorist who articulated the principles of Jeffersonianism in perhaps their most ideal form.[8] Taylor's analysis, like that of Madison and Adams, focused sharply on the economic issue of unequal distribution of wealth. Taylor, however, in contrast to Adams and Hamilton, denied that inequality is inevitable. As Beard wrote:

> At the outset of his plea for a republic based upon substantial equality, Taylor is compelled to face Adams' fundamental proposition that such a system of government is impossible because the sources of inequality "are founded in the constitution of nature," and cannot be eradicated no matter what institutional devices are invented.... He [Taylor] simply denies its validity.[9]

In Taylor's view, inequality is the result of exploitation, not superior virtue.

> He [Taylor] will not admit that the great differences in wealth, the abysmal division into rich and poor, are historically the product of the industry of the few and the sloth of the many. On the contrary, he holds

---

15. As Charles Warren put it, "[T]he great struggle for the Presidency in the fall of 1800 ... resulted in the overthrow of the Federalist Party and ... produced a complete revolution in the political trend of the country...." 1 Warren, *The Supreme Court*, 168.

7. Columbian Centinal, Aug. 27, 1800, quoted in Beard, *Jeffersonian Democracy*, 360. Beard wrote, "In the field of federal law and politics, the conflict between the Republicans and the Federalists was over economic issues and not over any mere adjustments of the constitutional system." *Id.*

8. Taylor is often referred to as "John Taylor of Caroline." The main source of this exposition of his ideas is Beard, *Jeffersonian Democracy*, 322–52. Jefferson "thoroughly indorsed Taylor's *Inquiry into the Principles and Policy of Government of the United States* ... and declared that Col. Taylor and he had never differed on any political principle of importance." Beard, *Jeffersonian Democracy*, 415 n.1.

9. *Id.*, 323.

that the older aristocracies ... were begotten ... by exploitation, not by thrift and savings.[10]

The specifically American form of aristocracy, according to Taylor, was based upon wealth achieved through manipulation of the financial system (stocks, bonds, currency, etc.). The remedy against exploitation by the financial oligarchy, he proposed, was to use the political process to destroy their special privileges.

Thomas Jefferson's politics were based on essentially the same principles as Taylor's. Jefferson shared Taylor's hostility toward the merchants, manufacturers, and financiers who were the leaders of Hamiltonian capitalism, and he made his political appeal to the masses of small farmers who comprised the most populous element of society.[11] To quote Beard once again:

> Jefferson's views on fundamental economic questions were not matters of speculation. In his *Notes on Virginia* he had denounced the arts of the merchant and the financier, and declared the landowning farmer to be the only hope of a republic. He had made it plain that the methods of capitalism were not only highly objectionable to him personally, but that, in his opinion, an extensive development of them was incompatible with the perpetuity of American institutions.[12]

Jefferson's political platform, however, was not based upon the concept of a powerful national government acting vigorously on behalf of the small farmer. His goal was to stop the national government from granting special privileges to the capitalist class and to return to a laissez faire system.

In this regard, it is important to recognize that, over the course of American history, economic conservatives and liberals have changed places on the issue of government intervention in economic affairs. During the nation's early years, conservatives such as Hamilton and Marshall favored a strong, active national government. Since, at the time, government was dominated by the wealthy, a strong government was then normally one that vigorously aided property owners. Concurrently, liberals such as Jefferson endorsed a laissez faire role for govern-

---

10. *Id.*

11. Jefferson's politics were not simply a matter of rich versus poor. His respect for the small farmer did not extend to the urban artisan. Thus, for Jefferson, the fundamental issue was the farmer against the city dweller, rather than the poor against the rich. Nevertheless, since most small farmers were not wealthy, the rich-poor issue was usually implicit.

12. Beard, *Jeffersonian Democracy*, 358.

ment in which special privileges were not granted to the wealthy. As the franchise spread and the ballot became a vehicle of political power for the masses, Andrew Jackson, Franklin D. Roosevelt, and other liberals favored strong government action on behalf of the poor, and conservatives such as Stephen J. Field, Richard Nixon, and Ronald Reagan came to support a policy of reducing regulation of the economy, particularly when the regulations restrict rich entrepreneurs and powerful corporations.

After their defeat in the 1800 election, the Federalists turned their hopes to the judiciary as the branch of government that might continue to carry out Federalist policies. One of President Adams' last important acts was to appoint John Marshall as Chief Justice and standard-bearer for the Federalist forces in the judiciary. When Jefferson took office in March 1801, nearly all the federal judges were Federalists. "[W]hile in possession of the Executive and Legislative branches of the Government, the Republicans had no representative in the Judicial branch.... [13] Since the Federalist judges were appointed for life, years would pass before the anti-Federalist faction could take over.

Jefferson understood the situation and wrote, "[T]he Federalists have retired into the Judiciary as a stronghold . . . and from that battery all the works of republicanism are to be beaten down and erased."[14] As it turned out, he never succeeded in breaking the Federalist hold on the judicial system.

When Jefferson was inaugurated, conservatives completely controlled the Supreme Court. Chief Justice Marshall was an economic conservative. For Marshall, the Court's duty to protect the rich was second in importance only to its duty to enhance the power of the Court and the federal government. The other five Justices supported Marshall's economic conservatism. Bushrod Washington was a conservative Federalist who allied himself closely with Marshall.[15] The volatile Chase was an ardent conservative during his Court tenure. Jus-

---

13. 1 Warren, *The Supreme Court*, 190. Warren continued, "[T]he distrust of the United States Courts by the anti-Federalists had been rapidly increasing during the past years; and the decisions and actions of the Judges, adverse to practically every cardinal Anti-Federalist doctrine, and supporting the political tenets of the Federalist party, had gradually caused them to regard these Courts as a mere annex of that party." *Id.*

14. *Id.*, 193.

15. Toward the end of his long career on the Court, Washington deviated from Marshall's economic conservatism in one important case: *Ogden v. Sanders*, 25 U.S. (12 Wheat.) 213 (1827). During the 1801–12 period, however, Washington was a reliable member of the conservative bloc.

tices Cushing, Paterson, and Moore were also conservative Federalists. In short, upon assuming the Presidency, Jefferson confronted a Supreme Court with a solid 6-0 conservative majority and his nemesis John Marshall presiding.

Despite the efforts of three successive Republican Presidents, Jefferson, Madison, and James Monroe, to change the situation, this dominance was not definitively broken until Marshall's death in 1835. Several factors combined to thwart Republican efforts to liberalize the Bench. First, Jefferson, Madison, and Monroe made only six Court appointments during their combined 24 years in office.[16] Marshall and Washington survived into the Jackson era. With the Court manned by only six Justices up to 1807 and seven thereafter,[17] the two needed only an additional pair of sympathizers among the remaining Justices to control the Court. The Republican appointments gave them more than needed.

From the perspective of anti-Federalist politics, Jefferson did not choose his Justices wisely. Only William Johnson (1804–34) made a decent showing on behalf of Jeffersonian concepts.[18] Both Henry Livingston (1807–23), a political and economic moderate, and Thomas Todd (1807–26), a Kentucky land lawyer, "promptly disappeared into the shadow of Marshall."[19]

---

16. Jefferson appointed William Johnson (1804–34), H. Brockholst Livingston (1806–23), and Thomas Todd (1807–26). Madison appointed Joseph Story (1812–45) and Gabriel Duval (1812–35). Monroe appointed Smith Thompson (1824–43). During the 12 years from 1812 to 1823, no Supreme Court appointments were made. This remains the longest period without appointments in Supreme Court history to date.

17. The seventh seat was created by federal statute in 1807.

18. For a detailed discussion of Justice Johnson, see D. Morgan, *Justice William Johnson* (1954). Johnson was the first Justice in Supreme Court history who had a substantial inclination toward economic liberalism. Although by no means radical, Johnson was more likely than the other Justices to grant federal and state legislatures broad power to legislate in the public interest at the expense of vested property rights. "From the outset, the young Jeffersonian judge had looked with deference upon the rights of property.... But Johnson found that the public too, had important interests in the law.... Provided its voice was clear and unequivocal, the national legislature might pass 'severe laws' in protecting the public interest." *Id.*, 208. Johnson's frustration with the Court of his early years is revealed by the following passage in his letter to Thomas Jefferson explaining why Marshall always wrote the lion's share of majority opinions: "Cushing was incompetent, Chase could not be got to think or write, Paterson was a slow man and willingly declined the trouble, and the other two Judges (Marshall and Bushrod Washington) you know are commonly estimated as one Judge." 1 Warren, *The Supreme Court*, 655.

19. Pfeffer, *This Honorable Court*, 41.

Madison's appointments made matters even worse for the Court's Jeffersonian wing. Maryland aristocrat Gabriel Duval (1812–35) was a reliable Marshall supporter. And Joseph Story (1812–45) turned out to be a strong conservative who gave the Marshall-Washington bloc a brilliant, scholarly mind and another consistent vote.[20] Story's role on the Supreme Court has been described as follows:

> Story was quickly and completely captured by (or, perhaps more accurately, surrendered to) Marshall. The relationship between them was somewhat like that between Boswell and Samuel Johnson, one not merely of deep affection but of hero worship.[21]

But we are getting ahead of our story. Let us return to Jefferson. Table 2 illustrates the conservative dominance on the Court after Jefferson's three appointees had been seated.

TABLE 2
Alignment of Justices, 1807–12

Left	Center	Right
	Johnson	Marshall
	Livingston	Washington
		Chase
		Cushing
		Todd

A second factor contributing to the continued Federalist control of the Court was the unusual dominance exercised by Chief Justice Marshall. Jefferson wrote, "It will be difficult to find a character of firmness enough to preserve his independence on the same Bench with Marshall."[22] As it happened, only Johnson met this specification, and he was simply overmatched by the Marshall-Washington bloc.

Finally, the failure of the anti-Federalists to capture the Court was partially the result of the failure of the Republican Party to generate a viable political program.[23] Once in power, the Jeffersonians turned out

---

20. Story was nominally a Republican, but he was conservative through and through in his economic, political, and judicial beliefs. At the time of his appointment, former President Jefferson warned President Madison that Story was a "pseudo-Republican" and not to be trusted. 1 Warren, *The Supreme Court*, 417.

21. Pfeffer, *This Honorable Court*, 41.

22. 1 Warren, *The Supreme Court*, 402.

23. This failure resulted from anachronistic qualities of the Jefferson political credo. Given the irresistible drive toward industrial development, it was simply not possible to maintain political power with an imagery and political program based on notions of an agrarian arcadia.

to be far from the radicals the Federalists had feared in 1800. Jefferson moved rapidly back toward the political center after his inauguration and was later followed there by Madison and Monroe. By the time Monroe took office, the Republicans had adopted many of the views of the old Federalists.

Given a series of surprisingly conservative appointments, Marshall's strengths, and the lack of a viable Republican political program, how was Jefferson able to hold the Supreme Court at bay?

The answer is that the dominant forces of Jeffersonianism mounted a sharp, effective attack on the Court during the early 1800's. First, the Justices were put out of business for 14 months during 1802 and 1803 by legislation ostensibly designed to change the dates of the Court's terms, but really intended to give the Court an involuntary vacation.[24] Second, an attempted impeachment of Justice Chase fell only four votes shy of success. This was a near miss for the Marshall Court. The Jeffersonians were pushing the principle that impeachment was proper not only for "high Crimes and Misdemeanors,"[25] but also whenever Congress disagreed with a Justice's views, and "it is an undoubted fact that, had the effort been successful, it was the intention of the Republicans to institute impeachment proceedings against all the Judges of the Court."[26] Third, Congress made repeated efforts to enact constitutional amendments and statutes stripping the Court of its power.

These events intimidated even Marshall, as is demonstrated by the following astonishing statement in a letter from Marshall to Chase:

> I think the modern doctrine of impeachment should yield to an appellate jurisdiction in the legislature. A reversal of those legal opinions deemed unsound by the legislature would certainly better comport with the mildness of our character than a removal of the judge who had rendered them unknowing of his fault.[27]

As a result, "Marshall's contribution to the evolution of the Court may lie as much in the decisions that he did not make as in those that he did. . . . Marshall was too prudent to present Jefferson and the Republicans with an all-out challenge at the height of their popularity and at the nadir of the Federalists."[28]

---

24. It has often been speculated that the Jeffersonians put the Court on vacation to prevent Marshall from deciding *Marbury v. Madison,* 5 U.S. (1 Cranch) 137 (1803).

25. U.S. Const. art. II, sec. 4.

26. 1 Warren, *The Supreme Court,* 293.

27. Pfeffer, *This Honorable Court,* 87.

28. *Id.,* 78.

Accordingly, Jefferson's failure to capture the Court did not make any great impact until after Jefferson left office. The Court did not, during Jefferson's tenure, impose major obstacles to economic reforms.[29] Instead, it stood passively aside as the Jefferson administration cut military spending, discontinued the production of war vessels, abolished excise taxes on whiskey, reduced the public debt, and carried out numerous measures to counteract "the right to use Government for the benefit of any capitalistic groups, fiscal, banking, or manufacturing."[30] The Marshall Court also upheld the statute repealing the lucrative positions of the midnight judges created at the last minute by the Adams administration.[31]

After Jefferson's 1809 departure from the presidency, the Supreme Court gradually began to take an activist role in support of economic conservatism, a trend whose emergence became apparent in *Fletcher v. Peck*.[32] This case, which has been discussed at length by many commentators, involved the Georgia legislature's corrupt Yazoo public land grants. In all, 35 million acres in the present States of Alabama and Mississippi were granted to syndicates of private investors at a bargain price. Thereafter wholesale bribery of Georgia legislators who voted for the grants came to light.

A later Georgia legislature passed a statute rescinding the grants. The speculators brought suit challenging the constitutionality of the rescinding statute and the litigation was carried to the Supreme Court. Although some small investors were involved, the case presented a classic rich-poor issue. It set syndicates of wealthy investors, largely from

---

29. Of course, the most famous case of all, *Marbury v. Madison*, 5 U.S. (1 Cranch) 137 (1803), was decided during this period. As repeatedly pointed out by commentators, however, the genius of the *Marbury* opinion was its assertion of the great principles of judicial review and government accountability to the rule of law in a context which did not require an order that Jefferson and his colleagues could disobey. The Court did not, during Jefferson's Presidency, attempt to take an activist role in the formulation of political and economic policy. As Pfeffer stated, "The only major decision that Marshall issued during the eight years Jefferson was President was *Marbury*." Pfeffer, *This Honorable Court*, 95.

30. Beard, *Jeffersonian Democracy*, 467. For a general discussion of the Jefferson administration's economic policies, see *id.*, 435–67.

31. The repeal of Adams' midnight judges act was challenged in litigation that reached the Supreme Court. In *Stuart v. Laird*, 5 U.S. (1 Cranch) 299 (1803), Marshall upheld the repealing statute, even though it reinstated the hated circuit riding requirement. The case provides a good symbol of Marshall's passivity during the period when the Court was under Jefferson's shadow.

32. 10 U.S. (6 Cranch) 87 (1810).

New England, against the people of Georgia. The Court ruled that the rescinding statute was a law impairing the obligation of contracts and hence void. The speculators kept their lands. More important, the contract clause was converted into the Court's most powerful weapon in its battle against economic reform efforts by state legislatures.

Fletcher v. Peck illustrates the 1810 Court's economic conservatism and suggests that Marshall and his Associates were finally ready to move out from under Jefferson's shadow and to assert their policies of nationalism and economic conservatism in an activist manner. Nevertheless, the case was an exception to the general pattern of judicial restraint that characterized the 1801–12 period, a pattern summarized by Supreme Court historian and Harvard Professor Robert J. McCloskey as follows: "[T]he Court after 1801 was for some time no more formidable than it had been before.... Marshall was holding back, awaiting a more propitious future."[33]

---

33. R. McCloskey, *The American Supreme Court* (1960), 40.

5
The Prime and Decline of John Marshall (1812–1835)[1]

Defeated in the open field by Jefferson, Federalism had retreated to prepared defenses. Under the resourceful leadership of John Marshall it entrenched itself in the courts of law and sought to make them unshakable bulwarks against change.[2]

In 1812, Supreme Court history took an ironic turn. Justice Cushing had died in 1810, and Justice Chase in 1811. After a delay of nearly 12 years, the Jeffersonians had the chance to obtain a majority on the Court. "[O]ld Cushing is dead," wrote Jefferson at the time. "At length, then, we have a chance of getting a Republican majority in the Supreme Judiciary."[3] Yet the Court that emerged after the appointments of 1812 was nearly as conservative as the Federalist Courts of the 1790's. Why?

From the liberals' perspective, Madison committed the equivalent of a chess player's queen sacrifice in selecting replacements for Cushing and Chase. The alignment on the Court as late as 1810 was five economic conservatives (Marshall, Washington, Chase, Cushing, and Todd) and two moderates (Johnson and Livingston). The deaths of Cushing and Chase reduced the conservative wing to three. If economic progressives had been appointed to fill the vacant slots, the conservatives would have been on the short end of a 4–3 split.

---

1. For an extended discussion of this period, see 1 Warren, *The Supreme Court*, 400–814. Marshall, of course, had been Chief Justice since 1801, but it was not until roughly 1812 that the economic conservatives recovered sufficiently from the Jeffersonian boom to reestablish their confidence and begin to move boldly.

2. Schlesinger, *The Age of Jackson*, 322.

3. 1 Warren, *The Supreme Court*, 403. In a letter to Madison, Jefferson wrote, "The death of Cushing gives an opportunity of closing the reformation, by a successor of unquestionable republican principles...." *Id.*, 404.

Instead, Madison appointed two more conservatives, Joseph Story and Gabriel Duval. The reason remains something of a mystery.[4] In Story's case, perhaps Madison was tired; his first three nominations for the spot had failed to receive Senate approval. In any case, the outcome is no mystery: Marshall's conservative wing retained control.

As previously mentioned, Story was a conservative who rapidly became John Marshall's strongest admirer.[5] Duval was also a generally conservative Justice who rarely disagreed with Marshall.[6] As a result, the Court that emerged in 1812 was, once again, composed of a solid five-vote conservative bloc and only two moderates.

TABLE 3
Alignment of Justices, 1812–23

Left	Center	Right
	Johnson	Marshall
	Livingston	Story
		Washington
		Todd
		Duval

The economic conservatism of this Court is not subject to serious

---

4. "The facts surrounding this [Story's] highly unexpected appointment remain a legal historical mystery." *Id.*, 415.

5. For an account of Story's career, see 1 L. Friedman & F. Israel, *The Justices of the United States* (1969), 435–53. Story's was "a conservatism in which property and contract became the central institutions from which all other values prescinded." *Id.*, 440. At the Massachusetts constitutional convention of 1820, for example, Story "was outspoken in his defense of vested rights and pleaded for virtual disenfranchisement of the urban working class." *Id.*, 446. According to Story, the main problem of government was "how the property-holding part of the community may be sustained against the inroads of poverty and vice." Schlesinger, *The Age of Jackson*, 269. Story was "highly obnoxious to Jefferson," who, in turn, referred to him as a "pseudo-republican" and "unquestionably a tory." 1 Warren, *The Supreme Court*, 406. "Jefferson's foreboding lest the new Judge should prove unsound on Republican political doctrines was justified; for within five years from the time of his appointment, Story had become an ardent supporter of the constitutional doctrines laid down by Chief Justice Marshall. ... " *Id.*, 419.

6. "Justice Duval generally supported Chief Justice Marshall's constitutional views." 1 Friedman & Israel, *The Justices of the United States*, 419. Duval disagreed with Marshall in only one significant constitutional case, *Dartmouth College v. Woodward*, 17 U.S. (4 Wheat.) 518 (1819). So complete was Duval's acquiescence that he filed only one dissenting opinion in his 22 years on the Court! Duval was a member of one of the wealthiest landholding families in Maryland.

dispute. As Justice Johnson's biographer put it, "The Court of John Marshall has acquired a reputation for extreme solicitude for vested rights. Its steady effort to shield from government interference the interests of property holders has become a byword to historians."[7]

The next few years presented Marshall with much more than a continued conservative majority on the Supreme Court. At the time, a shift in the nation's economic and political mood ushered in the "propitious future" he had been awaiting and set the stage for a period of conservative activism. Thus 1812 is as good a point as any to label the beginning of "the prime of John Marshall."[8]

The War of 1812 gave a substantial boost to the youthful capitalist system that had been nurtured by Hamilton. "[W]ith the end of the war came the turning of the attention of the American people from agriculture and shipping to manufactures. . . . "[9] The burst of industrial development that accompanied the war emphasized a point that was becoming increasingly apparent to all: the agrarian arcadia of Jefferson's dreams was simply not going to be. America's future would be one of industrial revolution and growth.

In addition, the voices of Henry Clay and Daniel Webster, the leading spokesmen of mid-century conservatism, were becoming stronger in the nation's councils. They espoused an "American system," an economic order based upon indigenous industry, financed by a vigorous national bank, and nurtured by protective tariffs. During their respective presidencies, Madison and Monroe could feel the wind changing and shifted increasingly toward political postures surprisingly akin to those of the old-time Federalists.

Few issues of major economic importance reached the Supreme Court until 1819. In that year, the nation experienced a major financial panic and the beginning of a severe depression that lasted almost a decade. Depressions normally lead to demands for economic reform and this was no exception. In three important cases decided in 1819, however, the Marshall Court made dramatic moves to contain the burgeoning economic reform movement and prevent it from hurting the rich.[10]

---

7. Morgan, *Justice William Johnson*, 207.

8. A case can be made, however, that the Marshall Court's activism began earlier. As we have seen, the 1810 Court had used the contract clause and the notion of vested property rights to declare unconstitutional the efforts of the Georgia legislature to recapture the fraudulent profits gained by land speculators in the infamous Yazoo land transactions. *Fletcher v. Peck*, 10 U.S. (6 Cranch) 87 (1810).

9. 1 Warren, *The Supreme Court*, 454.

10. In 1818, Story described the three cases as follows: "The next Term of the Su-

The first was *Sturges v. Crowninshield*,[11] a much-discussed case that dramatically illustrates Marshall's unwillingness to allow relief legislation to harm creditors. Because of Congress' failure to exercise its authority to enact a national bankruptcy act,[12] a number of States moved to protect their debtors by passing their own. In *Sturges*, a New York bankruptcy law was held unconstitutional as applied to contracts executed prior to the measure's enactment. Speaking for the Court, Marshall concluded that the New York statute violated the contract clause. Moreover, his opinion suggested that all state bankruptcy laws, if challenged before the Bench, would similarly be held unconstitutional, including those applying to contracts executed after their passage.[13] This was a frontal attack on one of the most central and recurrent economic reform demands, namely statutes allowing debtors, in hard times, to deviate from the terms of their contracts. As in *Fletcher v. Peck*, Marshall "exalted the constitutional contract clause as a barrier against relief legislation."[14]

The second landmark decision of 1819 was *McCulloch v. Maryland*.[15] In this case, Marshall gave urgently needed shelter to the Bank of the United States, a financial institution that was the central pillar in the Hamiltonian scheme of government-protected industry. This "hated banking corporation"[16] had lapsed in 1811, having become "an object of general odium, due partly to the fact that it was under almost complete control of the Federalists. . . . "[17] Over intense opposition, the bank was rechartered in 1816 during the nationalistic euphoria of the era of good feelings. "Within two years, however, by reason of bad management and mistaken policies, which had first encouraged overexpansion of credits and later drastically curtailed them, thereby ruin-

---

preme Court will probably be the most interesting ever known. Several great constitutional questions, the constitutionality of the insolvent laws, of taxing the Bank of the United States, and of the Dartmouth College new charter, will probably be splendidly argued." 1 Warren, *The Supreme Court*, 481.

11. 17 U.S. (4 Wheat.) 120 (1819).

12. U.S. Const. art. I, sec. 8 states, "The Congress shall have Power . . . to establish uniform Laws on the subject of Bankruptcies throughout the United States. . . . "

13. This dictum was later repudiated, over Marshall's dissent, in *Ogden v. Sanders*, 25 U.S. (12 Wheat.) 135 (1827), discussed below.

14. Morgan, *Justice William Johnson*, 117. "The serious effect of the decision upon the business community was heightened by the fact that the country was passing through a period of financial disaster." 1 Warren, *The Supreme Court*, 497.

15. 17 U.S. (4 Wheat.) 316 (1819).

16. 1 Warren, *The Supreme Court*, 504.

17. *Id.*

ing many State banks, the Bank had brought upon itself the intense hatred of the whole South and West."[18]

When the crash of 1819 occurred, "the general public placed the responsibility on that 'monster,' the Bank of the United States."[19] Legislation designed to break the Bank's power was passed in many States, including a heavy Maryland tax on all notes issued by the Bank within that State. Litigation concerning the Maryland tax was carried to the Supreme Court, where Marshall, adopting the arguments of the Bank's celebrated attorneys, Daniel Webster, William Pinckney, and William Wirt, held that tax unconstitutional.

The most important aspect of Marshall's opinion was his broad reading of the Constitution's "necessary and proper" clause[20] to confer upon Congress broad discretion to select whatever means are convenient for exercising its delegated powers. Although the power to create a bank is not explicitly mentioned in the Constitution, Marshall held that it is implied, since Congress might conclude that the use of a corporation is convenient for carrying out its fiscal powers. Having found that Congress had the power to charter a bank, Marshall proceeded to hold that the supremacy clause[21] bans States from taxing the Bank of the United States.

The *McCulloch* opinion was vintage Marshall. In a single stroke, he vastly augmented the power of the national government, restricted the power of the States, and protected powerful pro-Bank interests. The Jeffersonians were outraged. Jefferson, Madison, and Spencer Roane, Virginia's ardently Republican Chief Justice, were furious. The Niles Register, a leading Republican newspaper, called the case a "judicial decision which threatens to annihilate the sovereignties of the States ... and make the productive many subservient to the unproductive few...."[22]

The third "great case" of 1819 was *Dartmouth College v. Woodward*,[23] which again used the contract clause to strike down reform efforts by Republicans.[24] Frustrated by the policies of the Federalist-dom-

18. *Id.*, 505.
19. *Id.*
20. U.S. Const. art. I, sec. 8.
21. U.S. Const. art. VI. The clause provides, "[T]he Laws of the United States ... shall be the supreme Law of the Land...."
22. 1 Warren, *The Supreme Court*, 523.
23. 17 U.S. (4 Wheat.) 518 (1819).
24. Both *McCulloch* and *Dartmouth College* were argued by Daniel Webster, one of the most successful and eloquent defenders of property rights in the history of the

inated board of directors of Dartmouth College, New Hampshire Republicans attempted to modify the college's charter and pack the board with Republicans.[25] Marshall thwarted this effort by holding, for the first time, that corporate charters are contracts within the meaning of the contract clause and that States therefore máy not enact laws impairing the obligations set forth in corporate charters. The case was a victory for vested rights.[26] Moreover, it laid down a doctrine of extremely far-reaching potential for protecting the corporations which were to become the basic organizational units of the American industrial system.

The Jeffersonians, naturally enough, were angered by the 1819 trilogy of conservative-activist rulings. Jefferson shared their dismay. In 1820, he wrote, "The Judiciary of the United States is the subtle corps of sappers and miners constantly working underground to undermine the foundations of our confederated fabric."[27] In 1821, he wrote to Roane, "The great object of my fear is the Federal Judiciary. That body ... is ingulphing insidiously the special governments into the jaws of that which feeds them.... Let the eye of vigilance never be closed."[28]

This 1819 trilogy of Supreme Court rulings was one of the most dramatic developments in the entire history of the Court's involvement in rich-poor controversies. It marked the first major instance of vigorous

---

United States. Here is Webster's head count after the *Dartmouth College* oral arguments: "The Chief Justice and Washington, I have no doubt are with us. Duval and Todd, perhaps against us; the other three, holding up. I cannot much doubt but that Story will be with us in the end, and I think we have much more than an even chance for one of the others. I think we shall finally succeed." 1 Warren, *The Supreme Court*, 480.

25. In a letter to William Plumer, leader of the New Hampshire Republicans, Thomas Jefferson summarized the economic issues at stake. *See id.*, 484–85. "[Jefferson's] letter marked the lines on which the political parties had begun to differ. The Federalists, in general, laid stress on the rights of property created by legislation and their inviolability as against subsequent legislative control, and they sought to protect vested rights against fluctuating public sentiment and the rapidly changing political condition of the times.... The Republicans, on the other hand, looked with suspicion on a doctrine which restrained the people from resuming control of franchises which the people had created and granted." *Id.*, 485.

26. As a state court judge later put it, "The practical effect of the Dartmouth College decision is to exalt the rights of the few above those of the many. And it is doubtless true that under the authority of that decision, more monopolies have been created and perpetuated, and more wrongs and outrages upon the people effected, than by any other single instrumentality of government." 1 Warren, *The Supreme Court*, 492 n.1.

27. 1 Warren, *The Supreme Court*, 546.

28. *Id.*, 546–47.

conservative judicial activism. Previously, the Federalist Justices had played a rather passive role in deciding economic disputes brought before them. Now, the Court's intent to intervene in the nation's political processes on behalf of the rich was clear. In a single term, the Marshall Court limited the power of the States to enact legislation on behalf of the poor and expanded the power of the federal government to enact legislation on behalf of the great financial powers of the nation. *Sturges, McCulloch*, and *Dartmouth College* revealed a Supreme Court that stood ready to erect constitutional barriers against economic reform.[29]

1819 marked the apex of Marshall's career as champion of property rights. That year's depression extended deep into the 1820's, troubling James Monroe's last term, making John Quincy Adams' presidency an agony for him, and leading at last to Andrew Jackson's 1828 election. One Jackson scholar described this period as follows:

> The eighteen-twenties were a decade of discontent, born in depression, streaked with suffering and panic, shaken by bursts of violence and threats of rebellion. Jefferson's despondency, the intricate anxieties of John Taylor of Caroline, the furious despair of John Randolph, reflected this unrest in the moods of weary elder statesmen. But its main source was the profound frustration of thriving and vigorous classes who felt the central government to be hostile to their needs and interest. The planters of the South, the workingmen of the North, those small farmers of the North and West unconvinced by Henry Clay, could not but have grave misgivings over the workings of the American system. It seemed to them, as it was belatedly seeming to Jefferson, a betrayal of the Jeffersonian promise of equal rights in favor of special benefits for a single class. . . .
>
> Under strong popular pressure many of the states passed "relief" legislation, in the form of stop laws, stays of execution, and the establishment of state banks licensed to issue millions in paper. "Relief," of course, simply produced further inflation, bringing back those happy times when "creditors were seen running away from their debtors, and debtors pursuing them in triumph, and paying them without mercy."[30]

---

29. The Marshall Court's activism on behalf of the rich did not by any means end in 1819. *See Green v. Biddle*, 21 U.S. (8 Wheat.) 1 (1823), which struck down a Kentucky law providing that absentee owners could not evict settlers without paying compensation to the settlers for improvements made to the land. Another illustrative case is *Craig v. Missouri*, 29 U.S. (4 Pet.) 410 (1830), which held that "loan-certificates" issued by the State of Missouri, to combat financial distress and panic, were unconstitutional "bills of credit."

30. Schlesinger, *The Age of Jackson*, 30–31.

The case which, more than any other, tells the story of Marshall's ebbing dominance is *Ogden v. Sanders*,[31] which carved the dictum out of Marshall's *Sturges v. Crowninshield* opinion by upholding a bankruptcy law that applied only to debts incurred after the enactment of the statute. When such a statute is in effect at the time a contract is made, the Court held, the contract incorporates the statute. Bankruptcy therefore does not impair the contract. Marshall, dissenting, would have held that the obligations of even such subsequent contracts cannot be impaired by state bankruptcy laws.

Ogden v. Sanders substantially weakened the contract clause as a barrier to economic reform by validating the application of reform legislation to later-executed contracts. It was not until the 1890's that the ground lost by the conservatives was partly recaptured when the Court adopted the concept that "unreasonable" reform legislation constitutes a deprivation of "liberty of contract" without due process of law. Professor Pfeffer has described the significance of *Ogden v. Sanders* as follows:

> *Sturges v. Crowninshield* was for all practical purposes destroyed by the Court in the case of *Ogden v. Sanders*. This was the first case in which Marshall suffered a defeat on a major constitutional issue, and his defeat was total. Even Bushrod Washington did not join him in his dissent. Marshall's dissent was bitter. The effect of the decision, he said, was to make "prostrate . . . inanimate, inoperative and unmeaning" a vital provision of the constitution "on which the good and the wise reposed confidently."[32]

The division on the Court in *Ogden v. Sanders* was indicative of the weakening of Marshall's hold on his Associates in the late 1820's. A solid 5–2 conservative majority existed on the Bench as late as 1823. The following year, Smith Thompson (1824–43) replaced Livingston.[33] Thompson was somewhat more liberal than his predecessor. In 1826, Robert Trimble (1826–28), a moderate, replaced the conservative Todd. With these changes, the conservative majority was reduced to 4–3.

---

31. 25 U.S. (12 Wheat.) 213 (1827).

32. Pfeffer, *This Honorable Court*, 110.

33. At this point, "The Chief Justice was seventy-one years of age; Duval was seventy-four; Washington was sixty-four; Todd had been long ill; Thompson was new to the position; the Court seemed unable to cope with the burden of its duties." 1 Warren, *The Supreme Court*, 676.

TABLE 4
Alignment of Justices, 1826

Left	Center	Right
	Johnson	Marshall
	Thompson	Story
	Trimble	Washington
		Duval

The defection of only one conservative was enough to give the moderates a majority. In *Ogden*, the defector was Bushrod Washington, and the result was a 4–3 victory for Johnson, Thompson, Trimble, and Washington over Marshall, Story, and Duval.

In 1829, President Andrew Jackson took office. His opportunity to reshape the Court was obvious. Three of the four conservatives, Marshall, Washington, and Duval, were aging. Yet Jackson did not push the Court rapidly to the left. The moderate Trimble died in 1828, and Jackson chose the rather conservative John McLean (1830–61) to replace him. Marshall's proxy Bushrod Washington died in 1829, and Jackson appointed Henry Baldwin (1830–44), an economic moderate to succeed him. This succession certainly weakened Marshall's forces. Jackson's third opportunity did not come until six years into his presidency, and, once again, Old Hickory picked a conservative Jacksonian, Georgia's James M. Wayne (1835–67), to replace William Johnson, Jefferson's most effective Justice. Although Jackson's first three rather conservative appointments slowed Marshall's decline, the Marshall-Story bloc was clearly less dominant than in its 1819 heyday.

By 1834, Marshall's power was going into eclipse. Here is how Charles Warren sketched the scene:

> The transition through which the Court was now passing was clearly shown at this Term by the difficulty which the Court experienced in deciding several important cases which had been pending for some time. Of the older Judges, Johnson and Duval were incapacitated and absent much of the time; and the new Judges, Thompson, McLean, and Baldwin, differed frequently from Marshall and Story. Consequently the Chief Justice at the close of the Term announced that the three constitutional cases—*Charles River Bridge v. Warren Bridge*, *Briscoe v. Commonwealth Bank of Kentucky* and *New York v. Miln*—then pending, would be continued. . . . [34]

---

34. 1 Warren, *The Supreme Court*, 789–90.

A final comment is appropriate here regarding the struggle between Marshall and Jefferson that played such an important role in the first conservative era of Supreme Court history. Clearly Jefferson won the early rounds. From 1801 to approximately 1812, Jefferson and his Republican forces succeeded in intimidating the Marshall Court. The Chief Justice's strategy during those years was to wait patiently and to avoid open clash with the executive and legislative branches.

Marshall won the middle rounds. After Jefferson left office in 1809, the national mood shifted toward the nationalism and economic conservatism that Marshall preferred. Marshall took advantage of the favorable social climate to write his personal views on many issues into law through a series of landmark cases culminating in the 1819 *Sturges-McCulloch-Dartmouth College* trilogy. Says Schlesinger:

> This long and superb series of decisions written by Marshall, or under his influence, had pretty well established the Constitution as a document which forbade government interference with private property, even on the ground of the public welfare.[35]

From retirement at Monticello, Jefferson sent out anguished protests, but Marshall clearly had the initiative.

Beginning with the crash of 1819, however, Marshall's dominance began to wane. *Ogden v. Sanders* suggests that Jeffersonian economic liberalism was, by the late 1820's, a force to be reckoned with once again. No doubt Jefferson would have applauded Marshall's decline enthusiastically, but by 1827 he was dead. Marshall had outlasted his old enemy, only to see final victory slipping away during his waning years.

Marshall died in 1835. Conservatives were distraught over Marshall's demise. "Great, good and excellent man!" wrote Joseph Story of him, "I shall never see his like again.... Providence grants such men to the human family only on great occasions to accomplish its own great end."[36]

Others were not so sad. The Republican press said a loud good riddance to their aristocratic nemesis. Even Charles Warren later wrote:

> [I]t must be admitted that the time had arrived when a change in the leadership of the Court was possibly desirable. For at least thirty-one out of his thirty-five years as Chief Justice, Marshall had been out of sympathy with the political views predominant among the people, and in-

---

35. Schlesinger, *The Age of Jackson*, 322.
36. 1 Warren, *The Supreme Court*, 803, 813.

spiring the statesmen at the head of the Government. Moreover, . . . he had possessed a highly conservative nature and mental attitude. In view of the changes and reforms which were now taking place in the economic and social conditions, and the liberalization of political sentiment and processes which was marking a new era in the country's development, he was clearly out of touch with the temper of the times and less fitted to deal with the new problems of the day than with the great constitutional questions of the past.[37]

Near the end of his life, Marshall grew pessimistic about the future of his political and economic principles and the nation he loved so well. From the grave, Jefferson, his old antagonist, seemed to be having the last laugh.

His pessimism notwithstanding, Marshall had built well. The battle between economic conservatism and liberalism was far from over in 1835. In that struggle, which has lasted to the present and which appears to be a perennial theme of Supreme Court history, the wily Federalist had given the conservatives major advantages and had delivered major setbacks to the liberals.

Part Three
The First Liberal Era (1836–1890)

6
The Jackson/Taney Period (1836–1864)[1]

The age of American history dominated by Andrew Jackson marked the first time that democratic sentiments became majority viewpoints on the Supreme Court. It has been said that in 1837, the year in which Jackson left office, "[T]he election of 1800 . . . finally caught up with the Supreme Court."[2] As a result of Jackson's appointments, a modified form of the Jeffersonianism that had captured the legislative and executive branches but not the Court in the first decade of the nineteenth century became dominant on the Court as well.

The 1828 election brought to power a group of men who were committed to making the government the servant of the common people rather than the protector of the wealthy and privileged. These men, under Jackson's leadership, rode into office on the wave of discontent produced by the prolonged depression that began in 1819 and gave the 1820's the name "depression decade."

The Jacksonians believed the hard times of the 1820's were largely the result of selfish and irresponsible conduct by the banking community. The Jacksonian political program was centered upon breaking the nearly sovereign power of the existing banking system in order to create a financial system that would act on behalf of the entire people rather than mainly on behalf of vested wealth. Probably the single greatest political event of the Jackson era was the veto of the United States Bank, the predominantly private institution that had exercised essentially unrestrained control over American high finance. This veto marked the climax of a "battle between antagonistic philosophies of government: one declaring that property should control the state; the other denying that property had a superior claim to government privileges and benefits."[3]

---

1. Major sources for this chapter include Schlesinger, *The Age of Jackson*, and 2 Warren, *The Supreme Court*, 1–357.
2. Pfeffer, *This Honorable Court*, 126.
3. Schlesinger, *The Age of Jackson*, 92.

In this struggle between the classes, the Jacksonians explicitly sided with the have-nots. Amos Kendall, Jackson's closest political advisor, summarized his faction's philosophy this way:

> In all civilized as well as barbarous countries, a few rich and intelligent men have built up Nobility Systems; by which, under some name, and by some contrivance, a few are enabled to live upon the labor of the many.... [These ruling classes] are founded on deception and maintained by power. The people are persuaded to permit their introduction, under the plea of public good and public necessity. As soon as they are firmly established, they turn upon the people, tax and control them by the influence of monopolies, the declamation of priest-craft and government-craft, and in the last resort by military force.[4]

The Jacksonians reversed the Federalist views on government and economics and held that the task of government was to restrain the rich in their assaults on the poor. Marcus Morton, who then served on the Massachusetts Supreme Court, expressed the radical Jacksonian position in the following statement:

> My opinion is that the danger most to be feared and guarded against is encroachment by the powerful upon the weak—and by the rich upon the poor—and not the reverse. My constant apprehension is that the weaker members of the community will be divested of, or restricted in their rights. The greatest vigilance is needed to protect the common mass of the community—the industrious, quiet, producing classes of Society—against the overbearing influence of the rich and powerful.... If I am not always found on the side of the weak against the strong, whether in reference to Government, corporations or people, it will be because I err in finding which that side is.[5]

The Jacksonian political revolution, in contrast to Jefferson's, succeeded in capturing the Supreme Court. This was due, in large part, to the fact that Jackson made as many appointments to the Bench in eight years as Jefferson, Madison, and Monroe made in 24.[6] The Jackson Jus-

---

4. *Id.*, 97.

5. *Id.*, 171.

6. The number was six. John McLean (1830–61) succeeded the moderate Trimble. Henry Baldwin (1830–44) replaced the conservative Bushrod Washington. James M. Wayne (1835–67) took over William Johnson's seat. Philip P. Barbour (1836–41) served only six years, but made key contributions during that time, including the important opinion in *New York City v. Miln*, 36 U.S. (11 Pet.) 102 (1837). John Catron (1837–65) was appointed to fill a newly created seat just before the end of Jackson's presidency. Most important, Chief Justice Roger B. Taney (1836–64) replaced John Marshall and led the resurgent Jacksonian wing for nearly three decades.

tices also received substantial support from the appointees of later Jacksonian Presidents Martin Van Buren and James K. Polk.

The first liberal era of Supreme Court history was ushered in by the 1836 appointment of Chief Justice Roger B. Taney. Taney's ascension to the Bench was important for at least three reasons. First, it gave Jackson's appointees, for the first time, a Court majority. Second, it marked the departure of the venerable Marshall. Third, it brought to the Court the most forceful and articulate champion of popular rights in its 45-year history.

Prior to 1836, Taney had been a central figure in Jackson's administration and one of its most consistent radical democrats.[7] He was selected to serve as Attorney General in 1831. As a member of Jackson's inner circle, he played a key role in the President's war against the dominance of the wealthy classes over American politics. He was a staunch opponent of the United States Bank. He strongly encouraged Jackson in the decision to veto the Bank's charter. He drafted the major portion of the veto message which Schlesinger says "burst like a thunderclap over the nation." The message stated in part:

> It is to be regretted that the rich and the powerful too often bend the acts of government to their selfish purposes. Distinction in society will always exist under every just government. Equality of talents, of education, or of wealth cannot be produced by human institutions. In the full enjoyment of the gifts of Heaven and fruits of superior industry, economy, and virtue, every man is equally entitled to protection by law; but when the laws undertake to add to these natural and just distinctions . . . to make the rich richer and the potent more powerful, the humble members of society—the farmers, mechanics, and laborers—who have neither the time nor the means of securing like favors to themselves, have a right to complain of the injustice of their government.[8]

---

7. Charles Warren wrote, "The difference between . . . Marshall and . . . Taney can be best understood by a study of the long series of letters of warm personal friendship which Taney sent to Jackson, between 1836 and 1844; for in them the former's sympathies with the broad rights of the people, as opposed to the individual rights of any monied or privileged class, are strongly set forth. . . . [A]s Taney wrote to Jackson, in 1838: 'In large commercial cities, the money power is, I fear, irresistible. . . . [W]hen men, who have families to support . . . are aware that on the one side they will be employed and enriched by those who have the power to distribute wealth, . . . they are very apt to . . . surrender the lasting blessings of freedom and manly independence for temporary pecuniary advantages. They forget the grinding oppression that awaits them from the power they are contributing to establish, as soon as it is firmly seated in the saddle and no longer needs their support.' " 2 Warren, *The Supreme Court*, 36–37.

8. Schlesinger, *The Age of Jackson*, 90.

Subsequently, after two Secretaries of the Treasury had refused to withdraw federal deposits from the Bank, Taney accepted an appointment to that position and withdrew the deposits. Taney's economic liberalism was the subject of the following comment which appeared in a newspaper at the time of his seating on the Supreme Court: "Mr. Taney is as sincere and thorough a Democrat as any in the country. . . . [H]e is a sound anti-monopoly Democrat."[9]

Conservatives were aghast at Taney's appointment. As Charles Warren put it, "The Taney appointment was received with gloom and pessimism by the Whigs. 'Judge Story thinks the Supreme Court is *gone*, and I think so too,' wrote Webster."[10] The Senate confirmed Taney 29–15, defeating the Whig opposition led by Webster, Clay, and Calhoun.

The liberal Taney's replacement of the conservative Marshall was only one component of the liberalization of Court personnel that began with Jefferson's 1804 appointment of William Johnson, continued during Jackson's presidency, and extended at least until 1845, when Story resigned.[11] For example, the same year Taney was seated, the conservative Duval was replaced by Justice Phillip P. Barbour, another Jacksonian Democrat who espoused the States' rights philosophy that was the heart of the liberal Jackson/Taney jurisprudence.[12] Table 5 gives a rough picture of the balance of power on the Court on economic issues after the seating of Taney and Barbour.

---

9. 2 Warren, *The Supreme Court*, 12. Benjamin R. Curtis, also a Supreme Court Justice and a very able constitutional lawyer, said of Taney, "His power of subtle analysis exceeded that of any man I ever knew . . . in his case balanced and checked by excellent common sense and by great experience in practical business, both public and private." *Id.*, 13.

10. *Id.*, 10.

11. As previously noted, Jackson's first three appointments did little to liberalize the Court. In 1830, the moderate Robert Trimble was succeeded by John McLean (1830–61), a conservative, and the conservative Bushrod Washington was succeeded by Henry Baldwin (1830–44), a moderate who later claimed to have stood alone against Marshall's conservatism when he first arrived on the Court. In 1835, the moderate William Johnson was succeeded by the rather conservative James M. Wayne (1835–67). Democratic nominees became distinctly more liberal starting in 1836, when Taney was appointed.

12. John Quincy Adams characterized Barbour as a "shallow-pated wildcat . . . fit for nothing but to tear the union to tatters." Quoted in Schwartz, *From Confederation to Nation* (1973), 13.

TABLE 5
Alignment of Justices, 1837

Left	Center	Right
Taney	Baldwin	Story
Barbour	Thompson	McLean
		Wayne

Sparks flew immediately. "Within ten days after the opening of [Taney's first] Term, the Court heard the final rearguments in the three celebrated constitutional cases which had been pending, one for six years and the others for three years—awaiting the existence of a full Court."[13] Before the term was over, the Court handed down a trilogy of important rulings that seemed to confirm the conservatives' forebodings.[14]

The most noteworthy of the three, the *Charles River Bridge* case, has been aptly described as the "symbol of the dawn of a new era" in American constitutional law.[15] It stands out in United States Supreme Court history as a true landmark decision that summarizes and embodies with unusual clarity a major turning point in the development of the law. The opinion, which was Taney's first in the field of constitutional law, revealed a new and radical spirit substantially different from the jurisprudence that had dominated the preceding quarter century.

The facts of *Charles River Bridge* were these. For 50 years, bridge transportation across the Charles River from Boston to Charlestown, Massachusetts, had been in the hands of an extremely profitable monopoly. A corporate charter of 1785 had granted to the Charles River Bridge Company authority to build and operate a toll bridge across the river. This company was controlled by a group of wealthy private owners. In 1828, the Massachusetts legislature, controlled by Democrats, chartered a second corporation, the Warren River Bridge Company, to build a parallel bridge that was to become free as soon as sufficient tolls had been collected to pay construction and operating costs. Although the original charter of the Charles River Bridge Company did not ex-

---

13. 2 Warren, *The Supreme Court*, 21.
14. *Charles River Bridge v. Warren Bridge*, 36 U.S. (11 Pet.) 419 (1837); *Briscoe v. Bank of Kentucky*, 36 U.S. (11 Pet.) 257 (1837); *Mayor of New York City v. Miln*, 36 U.S. (11 Pet.) 102 (1837). The importance of the three cases is demonstrated by the fact that they occupy four hundred pages in the United States Reports.
15. Pfeffer, *This Honorable Court*, 123.

plicitly grant a permanent monopoly, the company brought suit to enjoin the new bridge.

The case presented in unusually clear form the question whether the law was to serve the interests of the rich or the poor: would the Supreme Court enjoin the people from providing themselves with free transportation in order to preserve the profits of a monopoly dominated by the few and the wealthy? The case for the Charles River Bridge Company was argued by Daniel Webster, who had worked with astounding success to ensure the primacy of property rights within the American constitutional system. Webster argued that the new charter impaired the charter rights of his corporate client by destroying the old charter's profitability and thus violated the Constitution's contract clause.

Rejecting Webster's arguments, the Court held that the people of Massachusetts could proceed with their toll-free bridge. Taney's opinion repudiated the contention that the legislature, in granting the corporate charter, had implicitly promised that neither it nor its successors would take any action which might reduce the corporation's profits. Speaking for the majority, Taney propounded his new image of government. The primary purpose of government, he said, is to promote the happiness and welfare of the people at large, not to protect the accumulated property of the wealthy few. When the two interests clash, it is not to be presumed that the good of the community must yield to the claims of the wealthy. As Taney put it:

> The object and end of all government is to promote the happiness and prosperity of the community by which it is established; and it can never be assumed that the government intended to diminish its power of accomplishing the end for which it was created. . . . A State ought never to be presumed to surrender this power because . . . the whole community have an interest in preserving it undiminished. . . . The continued existence of a government would be of no great value, if by implications and presumptions, it was disarmed of the powers necessary to accomplish the ends of its creation; and the functions it was designed to perform, transferred to the hands of privileged corporations.[16]

Pfeffer has described the importance of this decision as follows:

> This is a great opinion, on a par with Marshall's greatest, although proceeding from a diametrically opposite political and economic predilection. . . . The prime purpose of government is no longer to protect private

---

16. *Charles River Bridge*, 36 U.S. (11 Pet.) at 430–31.

property and promote profit-making (as it was in the philosophy of Hamilton, Marshall and practically all the fifty-five men who wrote the Constitution); it is now to promote the welfare of the community. The decision in favor of the free public bridge against the private profit-making bridge is one of the constitutional foundations of the social welfare legislation of the twentieth century.[17]

The significance of the case was also not lost on Justice Story, who felt that the decision amounted almost to a repeal of the Constitution, since the fundamental purpose of the Constitution was, in his view, precisely to protect the rights of the wealthy from this sort of attack. Story wrote to his wife, "A case of grosser injustice or more oppressive legislation never existed."[18] No doubt the case would have gone the other way in Marshall's prime. Indeed, the case had been argued before Marshall's death, and all three pre-Jacksonian Justices (Marshall, Story, and Thompson) were prepared to hold the new charter unconstitutional.

Briscoe v. Bank of Kentucky,[19] the second of the 1837 trilogy, also vividly demonstrated the economic liberalism of the early Taney Court. A Kentucky statute had authorized the issuance of promissory notes by a State-owned bank, the very kind of inflationary relief legislation that had been anathema to conservatives since the days of the Articles of Confederation. The issue was whether the notes were "bills of credit" prohibited by the Constitution.[20] The Court held the notes were not bills of credit. The decision provided breathing room for the States in their efforts to combat the severe depression that had begun in 1837. Story dissented. He concluded that the Kentucky notes, like the loan certificates in *Craig v. Missouri*,[21] were unconstitutional.

Mayor of New York City v. Miln,[22] the last of the 1837 trilogy, also illustrated the Court's new economic liberalism. A New York statute required ship masters to submit to customs officials lists of all passengers in order to assist New York with problems concerning foreign paupers. The Marshall Court's normal position was that local regulation

---

17. Pfeffer, *This Honorable Court*, 125.

18. 2 Warren, *The Supreme Court*, 24 n.1. "Webster wrote: 'The decision of the Court will have completely overturned, in my judgment, a great provision of the Constitution.' " *Id.*

19. 36 U.S. (11 Pet.) 257 (1837).

20. U.S. Const. art. I, sec. 10 provides, "No State shall ... emit Bills of Credit...."

21. 29 U.S. (4 Pet.) 410 (1830). *See supra* note 29, chapter 5, and accompanying text.

22. 36 U.S. (11 Pet.) 102 (1837).

of such matters should be restricted in order to minimize interference with interstate commerce. The Taney Court, on the contrary, upheld the local regulation. Speaking through Justice Barbour, the Court concluded that a State has "not only the right, but the bounden and solemn duty . . . to advance the safety, happiness, and prosperity of its people, and to provide for its general welfare, by any and every act of legislation, which it may deem to be conducive to these ends. . . ."[23]

This 1837 trilogy merits careful attention. Like its 1819 predecessor (*Sturges-McCulloch-Dartmouth College*), it symbolizes a particular era of Supreme Court history. Each of the three was a "great long-pending constitutional case" that had troubled the Court for years.[24] Each raised the basic issue of government power to regulate economic affairs. In each, the Taney Court adhered to the liberal line. "In all three of these cases, Judge Story dissented, and stated that Marshall before his death concurred with his [Story's] views."[25]

In the years following *Charles River, Briscoe,* and *Miln,* the liberalization of the Court's Justices continued. In 1838, two economic liberals, John Catron (1838–65) and John McKinley (1838–52), were sworn in to fill new, congressionally created seats. Catron was an acknowledged opponent of "accumulated wealth and privilege."[26] McKinley's anti-corporation populism was demonstrated by his noted circuit court decision holding that corporations could only do business in the State in which they were chartered.[27]

In 1841, the rather liberal Barbour was replaced by Peter V. Daniel (1841–60), who proved to be the most radical member of the Jacksonian wing.[28] Daniel was "the Court's extreme agrarian, the sworn en-

---

23. *Id.,* 139. Admittedly the outcome of *Miln,* giving local officials more power to detect and exclude paupers, was not especially liberal, but the same power to legislate in the commercial field would later be used to achieve more liberal ends. Moreover, the Court's language, like that in *Charles River Bridge,* was worlds apart from the Marshall-Story view and revealed a Court ready to uphold government action designed to achieve economic reform.

24. 2 Warren, *The Supreme Court,* 27.

25. *Id.*

26. 1 Friedman & Israel, *The Justices of The United States,* 748–49.

27. The Supreme Court decision in this case was captioned *Bank of Augusta v. Earle,* 38 U.S. (13 Pet.) 519 (1839), a landmark in its own right.

28. Daniel illustrates the often noted fact that the political spectrum is more like a horseshoe than a straight line and that radicals of the left and right often are quite similar. From the standpoint of Jacksonian anti-bank, anti-corporation economics, Daniel was arguably the Court's most left-leaning member. Daniel has also been viewed, however, as a conservative member of the Virginia planter group that advocated by-then reactionary agrarian political economics.

emy of . . . corporations, and banks; the extreme defender of states rights. . . . "[29] He believed that banks were "the most vicious example of great corporate monopolies, cancerous growths which would destroy the country if not cut out,"[30] and he advocated complete abolition of banks. His tenure on the Court was characterized by a consistent "opposition to any appeasement of corporations."[31] Table 6 shows the Court's liberal orientation after the seating of Daniel.

TABLE 6
Alignment of Justices, 1841

Left	Center	Right
Daniel	Baldwin	Story
Taney	Thompson	McLean
McKinley		Wayne
Catron		

By 1843, Joseph Story was the only Justice remaining on the Court from the era of Marshall and the Federalists. Story, it will be recalled, was an economic conservative who believed that government's main purpose was protecting property holders against "poverty and vice."[32] He had watched the development of Jacksonian doctrines on the Bench with a growing feeling that the Constitution was dead and the nation headed for doom as well. Story put it this way, "I am the last of the old race of Judges. I stand their solitary representative with a pained heart and a subdued confidence. . . . "[33] In a letter to a friend, Story wrote: "I am the last member now living of the old Court, and I cannot consent to remain where I can no longer hope to see those doctrines recognized and endorsed. For the future, I must be in a dead minority of the Court, with the painful alternative of either expressing an open dissent from the opinions of the Court, or by my silence, seeming to acquiesce in them."[34]

Hindsight tells us that Story's forebodings, like those of Webster, New York's conservative Chancellor Kent, and the aging Marshall of the prior decade, were unduly gloomy. Nevertheless, they show that the Court's democratic jurisprudence was fully recognized and deplored

---

29. 1 Friedman & Israel, *The Justices of the Unites States*, 800.
30. *Id.*, 797.
31. Schlesinger, *The Age of Jackson*, 329.
32. *See supra* note 5, chapter 5.
33. 2 Warren, *The Supreme Court*, 140.
34. *Id.*, 139–40.

by the wealthy classes and their partisans. When Story was replaced by
Levi Woodbury (1845–51), the Jacksonian revolution in Court personnel was essentially complete.[35]

With Taney and his fellow Jacksonians solidly entrenched on the Supreme Court, the legal concept that provided the keynote of the emerging democratic jurisprudence was the "police power." According to
this doctrine, governments have inherent power to promote the health,
safety, morals, and welfare of their citizens. Under Marshall, the police
power was construed narrowly in order to protect property rights. Under Taney, the Court granted the legislative and executive branches
much more latitude to exercise police power, and the Court more frequently rejected claims that state action illegally infringed the vested
rights of the wealthy.[36]

The significance of the police power concept has been described as
follows:

> [T]he police power concept was not invented by Taney or his Court; it
> was known in Marshall's day. But then it was understood narrowly, as
> its name indicates, to refer to the power of states to preserve order and
> safety within their borders. Under Taney the idea was broadened consid-
> erably to encompass the general well-being of the people; it became a
> power to provide for the welfare of the community. But not only was the
> scope of the concept widened; equally important, it was accorded a high
> constitutional status. As the opinions in the *Charles River* and *Miln*
> cases indicate, even if exercise of the police power transgresses on some
> other constitutionally protected right, such as the right to the fulfillment
> of the obligation of contract or to engage in interstate commerce, it is
> not for that reason unconstitutional. Implicit in this is the assumption

---

35. Prior to his appointment, Levi Woodbury was a member of Jackson's cabinet
and a supporter of both the Bank veto and the withdrawal of federal deposits.

36. Charles Warren wrote, "But Taney differed from Marshall in one respect very
fundamentally, and this difference was clearly shown in the decisions of the
Court.... Marshall was, as his latest biographer has said, 'the Supreme Conservative;'
Taney was a Democrat in the broadest sense, in his beliefs and sympathies. Under Marshall, 'the leading doctrine of constitutional law during the first generation of our National history was the doctrine of vested rights.' ... Under Taney, however, there took
place a rapid development of the doctrine of the police power, 'the right of the State
Legislature to take such action as it saw fit, in the furtherance of the security, morality
and general welfare of the community, save only as it was prevented from exercising its
discretion by very specific restrictions in the written Constitution.' ... It was this
change of emphasis from vested, individual property rights to the personal rights and
welfare of the general community which characterized Chief Justice Taney's Court."
Id., 34–35.

that not merely are the interests of the community superior to the rights of the individual, but also that the protection of private property and the promotion of profit making are not necessarily the only or even highest and overriding ends of government—an assumption completely alien to the philosophy of Hamilton, Jay, and Marshall.[37]

There were limits, however, to the scope of the Supreme Court's Jacksonian revolution. Conservative fears of the Bench's populist spirit were in large measure misplaced. When the dust stirred up by the 1837 trilogy settled, it became apparent that the Taney Court had not thrown property rights into the fire. On the contrary, among the Taney Court's major achievements was that its Jacksonian Justices were able to pursue their more democratic goals while maintaining substantial continuity with the Marshall Court's doctrines. As Court historian Robert G. McCloskey has pointed out:

> The legend of Taney and his brethren as radical democrats, hostile to property rights, nationalism, and Marshall's memory was stronger than the facts that would have emerged from a reading of the decisions themselves. But as the decisions finally were read and compared with those of Marshall's time, as the whole doctrinal course of the Taney Court was traced, it became apparent that the legend was badly misleading. The old jurisprudence had not been broken down after all, or even very greatly altered: the claims of property were still well protected, the nation was not constitutionally fragmented, judicial power was not surrendered.[38]

A decision illustrating the continuity between the Marshall and Taney Courts, and the latter's residual economic conservatism, is *Bronson v. Kinsie*.[39] Supreme Court historian Charles Warren has supplied a detailed description of the case's background.

> [A] recent statute of Illinois provided that a mortgagor's equity should not be lost for twelve months after foreclosure sale and that no sale should occur unless two thirds of the appraised value should be bid for the property. This was one of the many statutes which had been the outcome of the frightful state of business and finance then prevalent. The country had just passed through the panic of 1837; it was in the midst of the era of State bank failures and of State debt repudiations; scarcity of hard money had destroyed the inflated value of property; men who had debts to pay were forced to dispose of their property at ruinous prices to the few who had money to buy. As a consequence of these conditions,

---

37. Pfeffer, *This Honorable Court*, 127.
38. McCloskey, *The American Supreme Court*, 82–83.
39. 42 U.S. (1 How.) 311 (1843).

State after State had enacted statutes for the relief of debtors, stay-laws postponing collection of debts, laws granting exemption from execution and foreclosures of mortgages.[40]

Here was a classic situation in which economic liberalism called for assistance to debtors in their time of dire need. Yet, in *Bronson*, the Taney Court held that the Illinois relief law was a statute impairing the obligation of contracts and therefore void under the contract clause.[41]

There are many reasons why the "liberal" Taney Court surprised its followers from time to time with conservative decisions. First, the Court tends to absorb its new members and remake them in its own image, particularly when the doctrines in question are the levers of the Court's own power. Furthermore, Marshall's prestige increased rather than decreased with his death, since he died a mere mortal and was thereafter canonized as a saint and a sage. Most important, the ongoing surge of capitalism was too strong to be restrained by any branch of government, and capitalism demanded protection and security for property. The Taney Court, therefore, represents neither the nadir nor the zenith in the Supreme Court's cooperation with the rich.

In addition, toward the middle of the 1800's, the Court's position on the rich-poor issue became complicated by the slavery issue that grew into a national obsession overshadowing all other topics. In this context, controversies affecting the rich and the poor, which had held center stage in the political arena, became secondary matters, and the boundaries of economic conservatism and liberalism blurred.

One major cause of this blurring is that the party of the "common people," the Democratic Party, which had been formed by Jackson after the House of Representatives stole the 1824 election from him, drifted into a pro-slavery southern strategy that weakened its position as moral leader in the arena of economic reform. At the same time, the progressive impulse passed increasingly to the Federalists' successors, the Whig Party, and later the Republican Party, groups which despite their anti-slavery views still tended to favor business interests.

The infamous 1857 *Dred Scott* case[42] amply illustrates this ambiguity. Here the Court's entire "liberal" wing (Taney, Daniel, Catron,

---

40. 2 Warren, *The Supreme Court*, 102.

41. For other examples of economic conservatism in the heyday of the Taney Court, see *Planters Bank v. Sharp*, 47 U.S. (6 How.) 301 (1848), which held a Mississippi banking statute to be an unconstitutional impairment of contract rights, and *Suydam v. Broadnax*, 39 U.S. (14 Pet.) 67 (1840), which restricted application of state insolvency laws.

42. *Scott v. Sandford*, 60 U.S. (19 How.) 393 (1857).

and Campbell), all of whom were Southerners, concurred in the reactionary decision denying that black people, free and slave, were citizens who could bring lawsuits and holding that the federal government had no power to prohibit the extension of slavery into new geographical areas. The Court's two most economically conservative members, McLean and Curtis, dissented.

Increasingly, as the years passed, the pro-slavery faction became wedded to a radical States' rights philosophy that was held to be the key to the survival of slavery. This commitment was so strong as to subordinate the Jacksonian Justices' economic liberalism and to lead to States' rights decisions even when the result favored the rich over the poor.

In spite of the ambiguities and distortions created by the slavery issue, however, it seems safe to conclude that, overall, the Court at mid-century continued the tradition of economic liberalism inherited from the Jackson era. Chief Justice Taney, leader of the Jacksonian wing, remained in office until 1864. Daniel served until 1860, and his replacement, Samuel F. Miller (1862–90), was an economic liberal. As late as 1860, the balance of power on economic issues still tended to reside in the Court's liberal wing, as Table 7 shows.

TABLE 7
Alignment of Justices, 1860

Left	Center	Right
Taney	Grier	McLean
Daniel	Nelson	Wayne
Catron	Clifford	
Campbell		

For these reasons, it is appropriate to consider the entire period from Taney's seating in 1836 to his death in 1864 as a "period" of Court history during which economically liberal policies inherited from Jackson usually dominated the Court.[43]

---

43. To make the story complete, here is a brief identification of other new Justices who arrived on the Court around mid-century. In 1845, the moderate Smith Thompson was succeeded by Samuel Nelson (1845–72), another moderate, who had been Chief Judge of New York's highest state court. In 1846, the moderate Baldwin was succeeded by Robert C. Grier (1846–70), a moderate. In 1851, the moderate Woodbury was succeeded by Benjamin R. Curtis (1851–57), a conservative Boston lawyer. In 1858, Curtis was succeeded by Nathan Clifford (1858–81), a moderate conservative.

Before turning away from this era, a final look should perhaps be taken at the two great Chief Justices, Marshall and Taney, since they embodied with particular clarity the two typical judicial attitudes toward the perennial economic and political struggle between the rich and the poor. For the conservative Marshall, one of government's main duties was to protect property rights against attacks by the poor. And he believed the judiciary's fundamental role in a constitutional democracy was to ensure that the masses could not, through their greater numbers at the polls, invade the vested rights of the wealthy few. For the liberal Taney, government's role was to promote the welfare of the community, the people, the masses. Where the interests of the wealthy conflicted with the good of society as a whole, those interests must be viewed with suspicion and must be construed restrictively. Pfeffer provides an able summary of this dichotomy:

> The best of all possible worlds would come about, in Marshall's philosophy, by rapid and boundless economic expansion. The surest way to achieve this is by allowing individual initiative free rein, and this can be done only by protecting property and property rights through forcefully restraining the predatory envy of the lower classes. To secure these ends governments are instituted among men deriving their just powers from the good, the wise and the rich. Taney, though also committed to the judicial protection of property rights, believed that "the object and end of all government is to promote the happiness and prosperity of the community." His ideas of the community and the obligations that government owes it were completely beyond Marshall's realm of contemplation. Taney made of the concept of police power, barely known and severely limited by Marshall, an invaluable instrument for the effectuation of government's obligation to the community and a vehicle for social welfare legislation. To Marshall the constitution and particularly the commerce and impairment of contracts provisions, sanctified Adam Smith's *Wealth of Nations*; Taney's development of police power, a term not even found in the Constitution, provided the principal constitutional basis for America's present modified welfare state.
>
> In short, Marshall was in complete harmony with the temper of the century of American history from the time of his death in 1835 until the coming of Roosevelt's New Deal, Taney with that of the twentieth century from the time of the coming of Franklin Roosevelt.[44]

---

44. Pfeffer, *This Honorable Court*, 162.

7

The Court During the Post-Civil War Industrial Revolution (1865–1890)[1]

The post-Civil War era was a period of tremendous industrial expansion in the United States. Industrial capitalism, of course, was not new to the nation. It had been systematically encouraged and protected by Hamilton and the Federalists. It got a strong boost from the War of 1812. And it was sufficiently developed by the 1830's to cause intense struggles over factory working conditions and employees' rights to bargain collectively. Nevertheless, the nation that emerged from the Civil War was still overwhelmingly rural and agricultural. During the post-Civil War era, the United States experienced its real industrial revolution, undergoing a period of extravagant economic growth nicknamed "The Gilded Age."[2]

The Civil War gave a tremendous lift to American industry, igniting a boom that lasted until 1873. Leading the surge were the railroads, which started prior to the war and expanded rapidly in the years after. Business enterprises of unprecedented size were undertaken and huge fortunes amassed by such men as Commodore Vanderbilt of the New York Central and the "big four" of the Southern Pacific, Crocker, Hopkins, Huntington, and Stanford. Favors granted by the corrupt Grant administration (1869–77), such as the notorious agreement that allowed two imaginative profiteers, Jim Fisk and Jay Gould, to corner the gold market in 1869, added to the boom and increased the enormous profits of the entrepreneurs.

---

1. Selection of the year 1865 as the start of a new phase in the Court's first liberal era is somewhat arbitrary. The primary justification is that the Civil War ended that year. In addition, Taney died the prior year, and the seating of his successor, Chief Justice Salmon P. Chase, marked the end of the revolution in Court personnel resulting from President Abraham Lincoln's five appointments. Major sources for material presented in this chapter include C. Magrath, *Morrison R. Waite* (1963); A. Paul, *Conservative Crisis and the Rule of Law* (1960); C. Swisher, *Stephen J. Field* (1930); 2 Warren, *The Supreme Court*, 358–689.

2. 2 R. Hofstadter, W. Miller & D. Aaron, *The American Republic* (1959), 94–123.

The surge of industrial development set in motion by the Civil War continued in spite of periodic panics and depressions. The post-war boom collapsed in the panic of 1873, which was followed by a depression lasting until nearly 1880. However, the depression strengthened already strong companies by driving weaker companies into bankruptcy. During the 1870's, for example, John D. Rockefeller put together his Standard Oil monopoly by destroying or taking over his competitors. Similarly, the recession of 1883 and the depression of 1893, while temporarily delaying industrial expansion, did not deflect it from its long-term upward course.

The industrial revolution had certain specific social and economic results which are pertinent to the present study. First, the rich (or at least some of them) became richer. Fortunes far exceeding any previously seen in the United States were rapidly accumulated. Industrial growth was accompanied by increased concentration of wealth and power. In many fields, competition was almost completely eliminated, leaving control over vital goods and services in the hands of small groups of private individuals. Second, the plight of the poor (particularly the urban poor) was exacerbated. Impoverished city dwellers, their ranks swollen by large numbers of immigrants from abroad and migrants from rural areas, lived a Dickensian existence working in subhuman conditions for near starvation wages.[3]

The widening gap between the rich and the poor gave rise during the late 1800's to increasing class tensions. In order to defend their interests and redress the balance of power, the poor turned increasingly to federal and state legislatures, seeking the enactment of laws to regulate corporations and protect the masses. Reform oriented political movements appealing to the poor grew in strength as the years passed. These movements periodically caused conservative backlashes and gave rise to political counter-movements whose leaders opposed reforms and even denied that many reforms could be legally undertaken.

The fundamental question posed to the Supreme Court by the reform movement was whether legislative regulation of business activities constituted an unconstitutional infringement of the liberty and property of persons conducting those activities. As Professor Robert McCloskey put it, "[S]ince the gravest problem facing America was government regulation of business, that problem gradually became the

---

3. *Id.*, 260–87. Protective laws such as unemployment insurance, disability compensation, and welfare, of course, did not exist.

major interest of America's constitutional court."[4] C. Peter Magrath, biographer of Chief Justice Morrison R. Waite (1874–88), summarized the emergence of the economic regulation issue in the post-war era as follows:

> There was, for one thing, the whole question of economic regulation. By 1874, the outline of modern American society had clearly emerged; urban and industrial, it revealed great disparities of wealth and poverty, while small groups of men, accountable to no one, controlled the banks, railroads, and industries which were the economic sinews of the new nation. As those at the bottom of the economic scale felt the burdens of irresponsible economic power, there came demands for public regulation. First to protest were the western farmers who believed themselves oppressed by the giant railroad corporations. Those to be regulated naturally fought back, attacking the regulatory legislation on many fronts, but especially in the courts. From this conflict came some of the Court's most significant and difficult decisions.[5]

The post-war Court adopted a generally liberal approach to the resolution of this fundamental economic issue, allowing the federal and state governments substantial latitude to carry out economic reforms. President Abraham Lincoln's appointees were largely responsible for this posture. As the Jacksonians began to leave the Court, the task of replacing them fell to Lincoln, who made five appointments to the Bench during his four years in office.

Lincoln's first three appointees were economic liberals. In 1862, the conservative McLean left the Court. He was replaced by the moderate liberal Noah H. Swayne (1862–81), a Quaker and prominent Ohio attorney. Then Samuel F. Miller (1862–90) was chosen to succeed Daniel. Miller, one of the giants of Supreme Court history, had been a country doctor before rising to fame as an Iowa attorney and leader of Midwest Republicanism. As a Justice, his opinions "reflected a hostility to corporate and financial wealth."[6] In 1862, Lincoln selected his Illinois friend, Eighth Circuit judge David Davis (1862–77), to succeed Campbell, who had resigned when his State seceded. Davis was Lincoln's most liberal appointee and the Court's most liberal Justice. His

---

4. McCloskey, *The American Supreme Court*, 104.

5. Magrath, *Morrison R. Waite*, 182–83.

6. *Id.*, 99. Miller's liberalism is illustrated by the so-called Municipal Bond cases, in which the Court, for a change, rejected economic regulation over Miller's dissent. *Id.*, 210–11. For a detailed account of Miller's life and thought, see C. Fairman, *Mr. Justice Miller and the Supreme Court 1862–1890* (1939).

career was characterized by "opposition to corporate and financial interests."[7]

Lincoln's remaining two appointees were more conservative. A year after Miller and Davis took office, Stephen J. Field (1863–97) was selected to fill a newly created tenth seat on the Bench. Field, another giant of Supreme Court history, had moved to California in the 1849 gold rush, drafted California's basic statutory codes, and served on the California Supreme Court. A liberal in his early life, Field converted to ultra-conservatism and became one of the most conservative Justices in the Court's history.[8] Next, after nearly 30 years of service, the economically liberal Taney died. Lincoln appointed as the new Chief Justice Salmon P. Chase (1864–73), whom Lincoln described as "about one and a half times bigger than any other man I ever knew."[9] Inexpert in the law and restive in his judicial robes, Chase turned out to be a mediocre Chief Justice and an economic moderate.

The Lincoln Court's liberal wing was further strengthened in 1870, when President Ulysses S. Grant appointed Joseph P. Bradley (1870–92) to succeed the conservative Wayne. Bradley, another superstar of Supreme Court history,[10] was an eminent East Coast corporate lawyer who "showed marked independence toward the corporate interests he formerly defended, frequently upholding economic regulation."[11] He aligned himself in most cases with Miller and the liberals rather than with Field and the conservatives. In 1870, Grant also chose William Strong (1870–80) to replace the moderate Grier. "The conservative Strong,"[12] another railroad attorney, sided with Field on most economic issues.

Table 8 summarizes the alignment on the Court after the seating of the Lincoln and Grant appointees.

---

7. *Id.,* 99.

8. When the relatively liberal Catron left the Court in 1865, he was not replaced, so the Court was reduced again to nine Justices. The Catron/Field "succession" was clearly a conservative change.

9. 2 Warren, *The Supreme Court,* 400. The reference was to Chase's character, not physical size.

10. "With his powerful intellect and moral assertiveness, he surpassed all but a handful of judges who have sat upon the Court." 2 Friedman & Israel, *The Justices of the United States,* 1200. "Bradley was later to prove one of the strongest members of the bench, on a par with Miller and Field." Pfeffer, *This Honorable Court,* 185.

11. Magrath, *Morrison R. Waite,* 100.

12. 2 Warren, *The Supreme Court,* 518.

TABLE 8
Alignment of Justices, 1870

Left	Center	Right
Davis	Chase	Field
Miller	Nelson	Strong
Swayne	Clifford	
Bradley		

Although the liberal wing lacked an absolute majority, it was clearly the strongest bloc.

The relatively liberal post-war Court's willingness to allow substantial legislative regulation of business was revealed in the *Slaughter-House Cases* of 1873,[13] the Court's first decision interpreting the critically important due process clause of the Constitution's fourteenth amendment, which had been ratified in 1868. At issue was a Louisiana statute granting a monopoly in the New Orleans slaughterhouse business to one corporation. Former Justice Campbell, who had resigned from the Court when Alabama seceded and had become an eminent member of the private bar, argued for petitioners that the due process clause should be construed to prohibit unreasonable regulation of business. The arch-conservative Field agreed.

But the Court, speaking through its liberal leader, Justice Samuel F. Miller, rejected the argument and adopted a narrow reading of the due process clause. Miller's explanation that the statutory restriction did not comprise a "deprivation of property" was unilluminating. Other cases of the same era, however, suggested that as long as economic reform legislation was enacted in compliance with proper legislative procedures, the Court's view was that it complied with the due process clause.[14] In other words, the due process clause was "procedural," not "substantive." And although the immediate effect of the *Slaughter-House Cases* was to preserve a hated monopoly, the liberal thrust of the decision was clear: the Supreme Court would not sit as a censor over economic reform legislation. The due process clause would not be construed as the source of power to nullify laws that the Justices might consider unsound or unreasonable.

During the same year in which the *Slaughter-House Cases* were decided, Chief Justice Chase died and Associate Justice Nelson resigned.

---

13. 83 U.S. (16 Wall.) 36 (1873).
14. *E.g., Davidson v. New Orleans,* 96 U.S. 97 (1877).

To replace Chase, President Grant chose Morrison R. Waite (1874–88). The Chase-Waite succession further strengthened the Court's liberal wing. Although he was an ex-business attorney, Chief Justice Waite normally voted to uphold economic reform legislation. Waite's biographer summarized his attitude as follows: "Dislike for the rapaciousness of the new capitalism, confidence in the people's capacity to govern, and a feeling that the function of judges was properly a limited one were, then, the judicial and social attitudes which shaped Morrison Waite's response in economic cases."[15] To fill Nelson's seat, Grant selected Ward Hunt (1873–82), another moderate. Hunt, a former New York lawyer and judge, was a minor figure in Supreme Court history. Perhaps his most notable achievement was serving five years while mentally incompetent, until a special law was passed allowing him to retire at full salary.

Table 9 shows the balance of power on the Bench during the crucial period in the mid-1870's when the Court developed its position on the emerging issue of business regulation. Clearly the liberals had the edge.

TABLE 9
Alignment of Justices, 1874–77

Left	Center	Right
Davis	Clifford	Field
Miller	Hunt	Strong
Swayne	Waite	
Bradley		

The question of the constitutionality of economic legislation was presented in its sharpest focus by legislation arising from the first major post-Civil War reform movement, the Granger Movement. This ferment, which began in 1867, was a collective effort by Midwestern farmers to check certain abuses of economic power by the railroads.[16] Fed by the social unrest caused by the depression that began in 1873, the Granger Movement succeeded in obtaining reform legislation in a number of States. One such "Granger statute" was an Illinois measure regulating the rates charged by certain grain elevators whose owners had obtained a stranglehold on the flow of grain from Midwestern

---

15. Magrath, *Morrison R. Waite*, 209.

16. The principal abuses were excessive and discriminatory rates. The remedies demanded by the Grangers were 1) maximum rate limits, 2) equal and nondiscriminatory rates, and 3) prohibition of monopolies.

farms to eastern markets. The elevator owners challenged the law as an illegal infringement of their liberty to conduct business as they saw fit and of their property interest in maximizing their business profits.

The case that settled the legality of regulating Chicago grain elevator rates, *Munn v. Illinois*,[17] is generally recognized by legal historians as the landmark case regarding the legality of economic reform legislation in the post-Civil War era. The Supreme Court, with only two dissents, upheld Illinois' authority to enact the regulatory legislation. Following the tradition of Taney and the Jacksonians, the Court based its decision on the States' police power and held that when private property is used in such a way as to create a public interest in its use, it may be regulated in order to protect that public interest.

The key passage in Chief Justice Waite's opinion for the Court is as follows:

> [T]he government regulates the conduct of its citizens one towards another, and the manner in which each shall use his own property, when such regulation becomes necessary for the public good.... Property does become clothed with a public interest when used in a manner to make it of public consequence, and affect the community at large. When, therefore, one devotes his property to a use in which the public has an interest, he, in effect, grants to the public an interest in that use, and must submit to be controlled by the public for the common good, to the extent of the interest he has thus created.[18]

This point was made even more forcefully by Justice Bradley in an outline he prepared to help Chief Justice Waite with the opinion.

> Whenever a particular employment, or a business establishment becomes a matter of public consequence so as to affect the whole public and to become a "common concern" it is subject to legislative regulation and control. Whatever affects the community at large ought to be subject to such regulation, otherwise the very object of legislative power—the consulting of the general good—would be subverted. Unrestricted monopolies as to those things which the people must have and use, are a canker in any society, and have ever been the occasion of civil convulsions and revolutions. A people disposed for freedom will not tolerate this kind of oppression at the hands of private corporations or powerful citizens.[19]

---

17. 97 U.S. 113 (1877).
18. *Id.*, 126.
19. Magrath, *Morrison R. Waite*, 182–83.

The Waite Court's economic liberalism was by no means limited to the issue of rate regulation. It was, according to biographer Magrath, a general characteristic of this Bench:

> In economic matters the Waite Court displayed indifference to the claims for special constitutional protection submitted by the nation's economic leaders. For one thing, its judges lacked any real commitment to the immense concentration of financial and corporate property which appeared after the Civil War. For another, all of the fourteen men who at one time or another made up the Waite Court (1874–89) grew to maturity in Jacksonian America, and most of them retained their democratic faith.[20]

As a result of their Jacksonian belief in regulating business to serve the public interest, the Waite Court Justices, as a rule, upheld economic reform legislation:

> Besides upholding state power to regulate railroads and alter the rights of creditors, the Waite Court sustained a variety of local regulatory laws despite claims that they violated the Fourteenth Amendment's due process clause, conflicted with the contract clause, or infringed on Congress' power over interstate commerce. Quarantine regulations, wharfage fees for public docks, prohibitions on the sale and manufacture of liquor, and condemnation of businesses that were a public nuisance all won judicial approval. Laws repealing earlier grants of monopolistic privileges were upheld in decisions taking a broad view of the states' police power.[21]

The United States' rising corporate elite looked upon these decisions with extreme disfavor. The following remarks—which, according to Magrath, may have been inspired by Field—demonstrate the intense reaction among representatives of corporate interests.

> No other decision [referring to *Munn v. Illinois*] has ever been made in the course of our judicial history,—not even excepting the notorious Dred Scott case,—which threatens such disastrous consequences to the future wealth and prosperity of the country.... [I]ts doctrine involves the very essence of the destructive theories maintained by the socialists and communists of France and Germany.... It is relied upon as an authority to sustain and validate the communistic legislation already enacted by several of the States.... [T]he step from the property of corporations to that of private citizens is a short and easy one; it will soon and certainly be taken, *for it has already been taken by the Supreme*

---

20. *Id.*, 205.
21. *Id.*, 215.

Court. The Dred Scott case indirectly struck at the stability of our political fabric; the Elevator case directly struck at the stability of private
property,—at rights which lie in the very foundation of modern society
and civilization.[22]

By 1880, dislike for the Court was already sufficient to foment an abor-
tive effort, backed by railroad magnate Gould, to pack the Court with
pro-business conservatives.[23]

Despite growing corporate opposition, the Court's relative economic liberalism continued into the 1880's. In 1877, the Court's most
liberal member, David Davis, resigned to pursue his political ambi-
tions, but he was succeeded by another liberal, John Marshall Harlan
(1877–1911). Harlan, a major figure in Supreme Court history,
promptly took over Davis' place on the Court's liberal edge.[24] Thus,
throughout Waite's Chief Justiceship, the proponents of economic regulation had four relatively reliable supporters on the Court: Miller,
Bradley, Waite, and Davis/Harlan. The liberal bloc normally could pick
up the needed additional vote and more from such moderates as William Woods (1881–89), Stanley Matthews (1881–89),[25] Horace Gray
(1881–1902),[26] and Samuel Blatchford (1882–1902). As Magrath put
it:

> Justice Stanley Matthews, while sympathetic to property rights, did
> not—as the business elite had clearly expected—join Justice Field in

---

22. Pomeroy, *The Supreme Court and State Repudiation,* 17 American L. Rev. 684,
712 (1883).

23. This phase of Court history has been chronicled in Magrath, *Morrison R. Waite,*
228–49.

24. Harlan was clearly the Court's most liberal member in civil liberties cases during most of his tenure. On economic issues, his performance was more checkered. He
frequently voted against labor's interests, for example. However, he also lined up with
the liberal wing on many rich-poor issues.

25. Matthews, an important member of the Court of his day, had an "unusual combination of liberal and conservative premises." 2 Friedman & Israel, *The Justices of the
United States,* 1351. "As a railroad attorney he defended business enterprise with logic
and passion. His conservatism did not, however, lead him to a denial of individual
rights." *Id.*

26. *See* 2 Friedman & Israel, *The Justices of the United States,* 1379–89. "His
[Gray's] prime interest was in historical developments in law. A lifetime dedicated to
this principle, coupled with great and consistent powers of work, made him conspicuous as a legal scholar and the most learned Justice of his generation." *Id.,* 1379. "Perhaps the greatest legal scholar on the Court was Justice Horace Gray. . . . It was suggested that his relation to Justice Miller was like that of Story to Marshall, that is, Gray
found a basis in legal history for Miller's intuitive decisions." W. King, *Melville Weston
Fuller* (1950), 132–33.

protest against the majority's "revolutionary course".... His [President Chester Arthur, 1881–85] two appointments to the Court, Samuel Blatchford and Horace Gray, neither of whom fit the railroad attorney model, also aligned themselves with Waite on the major economic issues before the Court.[27]

Meanwhile, the nation continued to polarize over the issue of government regulation of business. Under the banner of Social Darwinism and laissez faire, conservative interests sought a free hand for the financial and industrial entrepreneurs, while the poor pressed for increased government control. The recession of 1883, while not as severe as the depressions of 1873 and 1893, gave rise to social unrest with renewed demands for reform. During this period the labor movement experienced a major surge. Social tension climaxed in 1886 when the Haymarket Square bombing left several dead and a large number wounded. Cries of anarchy and communism were again heard.

But the Court did not yet swing to the right. In 1887, for example, _Mugler v. Kansas_[28] upheld a Kansas prohibition law as a valid exercise of police power. In his opinion for the majority, Harlan stated, "Under our system that power is lodged with the legislative branch of government. It belongs to that department to exert what are known as the police powers of the State, and to determine, primarily, what measures are appropriate or needful for the protection of the public morals, the public health, or the public safety."[29] This liberal view of police power was again evident in _Powell v. Pennsylvania_,[30] which upheld a state statute banning the sale of margarine.

During the 1870's and 1880's, opposition on the Bench to economic regulation came predominantly from Justice Field. In his view, most attempts to regulate the conduct of business were reprehensible and unconstitutional invasions of the sacred rights of liberty and property.[31]

---

27. Magrath, _Morrison R. Waite_, 247.
28. 123 U.S. 623 (1887).
29. _Id._, 660–61.
30. 127 U.S. 678 (1888).
31. Field's biographer summarized Field's views on these matters as follows: "Again and again he stressed the importance of great corporations in the achievement of things that were worth while. Because of their importance he insisted upon their being protected to the full extent of the law. Nothing stirred his ire more quickly than short-sighted efforts to restrict corporate activities. Such efforts were, in his estimation, of a piece with the dictates of the vicious doctrines of socialism and communism, and it was the duty of the courts to bring about their frustration. Yet his interest seems not to have been in corporations as such, but rather in the achievements of men of vision

Field's solicitude for the rich is revealed in numerous passages from his opinions. The following quotation, taken from his 1895 opinion denying the constitutionality of the federal income tax, is but one of many typical examples of his outlook.

> The present assault on capital is but the beginning. It will be but the stepping-stone to others, larger and more sweeping, till our political contests will become a war of the poor against the rich; a war constantly growing in intensity and bitterness. If the Court sanctions the power of discriminating taxation, and nullifies the uniformity mandate of the Constitution, it will mark the hour when the sure decadence of our government will commence.[32]

Field, with some support from Justice Strong and, occasionally, others, carried on a bitter and relentless fight against the Court's majority, a fight which finally succeeded in the 1890's when, with new personnel, the Court reversed itself and adopted Field's views.

In the twilight years of the period of judicial history that began in the days of Andrew Jackson and Roger B. Taney, and that we have labelled the Supreme Court's first liberal era, *Budd v. New York*[33] symbolizes both the state of existing law on the rich-poor issue and the changes impending in the Justices' attitudes. In *Budd*, the Waite Court's economic liberalism still prevailed, but only over the increasing opposition of the men who would soon provide the *dramatis personae* in one of the most significant Court turnabouts since 1790 and until the present.

The case involved a challenge to an 1888 New York rate regulation statute that set maximum rates to be charged by warehouses, grain elevators, and shippers along the crucial Erie Canal-Hudson River transportation system. The case was directly within the rule established by *Munn v. Illinois*. However, when heard earlier in the New York Court of Appeals, which upheld the law, a remarkable dissenting opinion was filed by Rufus W. Peckham, who only a few years later was to become a United States Supreme Court Justice. Here is what Peckham wrote:

> To uphold legislation of this character is to provide the most frequent opportunity for arraying class against class; and, in addition to the or-

---

and energy who used corporations as tools. His opposition, with but occasional exceptions, was to government interference with freedom of action in the business world. When business and industrial leaders garnered rich rewards for their labors, Field was ready to use the machinery of the law to protect them against the resentment and cupidity of the masses." Swisher, *Stephen J. Field*, 396.

32. *Pollock v. Farmers' Loan & Trust Co.*, 157 U.S. 429, 607 (1895).

33. 143 U.S. 517 (1892).

dinary competition that exists throughout all industries, a new competition will be introduced, that of competition for the possession of the government....

In my opinion, the court should not strain after holding such species of legislation constitutional. It is so plain an effort to interfere with what seems to be the most sacred rights of property and individual liberty of contract that no special intendment in its favor should be indulged in....

The legislation under consideration is not only vicious in its nature, communistic in its tendency, and, in my belief, wholly inefficient to permanently attain the result aimed at, but, for the reasons already given, it is an illegal effort to interfere with the lawful privilege of the individual to seek and obtain such compensation as he can for the use of his own property.[34]

Similar sentiments would not have been surprising coming from Field, but when *Budd* reached the Supreme Court, it was a new Justice, Field's nephew David Brewer (1890–1910), who picked up Peckham's themes. Declaring in his dissent that the rule of *Munn v. Illinois* was "radically unsound,"[35] Justice Brewer stated:

The paternal theory of government is to me odious. The utmost liberty to the individual and the fullest possible protection to him and his property is both the limitation and the duty of government. If it may regulate the price of one service, which is not a public service, or the compensation for the use of one kind of property, which is not devoted to a public use, why may it not with equal reason regulate the price of all service, and the compensation to be paid for the use of all property? And if so, "Looking Backward," [Edward Bellamy's radical, utopian novel] is nearer than a dream.[36]

Despite the thunderings of Peckham, Brewer, and Field, the Supreme Court upheld the New York rate regulation statute by a 6–3 vote. Thus, as late as 1892, Taney's concept of police power still prevailed over the emerging concept of liberty of contract. But the voices of dissent were growing louder and stronger.

---

34. 117 N.Y. 68, 69–71, 22 N.E. 670, 694–95 (1889).
35. Justice Field, of course, concurred in Brewer's dissent.
36. *Budd v. New York*, 143 U.S. 517, 551 (1892) (Brewer, J. dissenting).

Part Four
The Second Conservative Era (1890–1937)

8

The First Age of Laissez Faire (1890–1905)[1]

The preceding chapter described the socio-economic patterns that emerged after the Civil War and typified America's industrial revolution. Industrial expansion and concentration gave rise to private businesses of unprecedented wealth and power. At the same time, urbanization, immigration, and industrialization produced a class of factory workers who lived in unprecedented poverty. To many observers, the traditional legal image of self-sufficient individuals dealing with each other in a context of independence and equality simply did not fit this new situation. Increasing demands were voiced for reform legislation designed to insure that private enterprise did not operate in a manner contrary to the public interest.

The traditional images, however, did not like old soldiers simply fade away. On the contrary, they took even stronger root among conservative groups that included the bulk of the rich and especially the entrepreneurs of the new industrial system. The politics of conservatism centered on the concept of laissez faire, the idea that government should keep its hands off business and let the economy go. This, in turn, was based on the twin pillars of Social Darwinism and Adam Smith's "invisible hand."

According to Social Darwinism, "survival of the fittest" is the mechanism by which the human race advances, and any attempt to ameliorate the struggle for survival by helping the weak and the poor would only lead to long-term harm. Moreover, Adam Smith's *Wealth of Nations* assured the Social Darwinists that self-interest, if left unregu-

---

1. The beginning and ending dates of this period are somewhat arbitrary. Clearly there was a conservative period during the last decade of the 19th and first decade of the 20th centuries. The starting point, however, could be placed as early as 1888 or as late as 1893, and the end could be placed as late as 1910. Useful sources for the material presented in this chapter include W. King, *Melville Weston Fuller* (1950); A. Paul, *Conservative Crisis and the Rule of Law* (1960) (hereafter cited as Paul, *Conservative Crisis*); C. Swisher, *Stephen J. Field* (1930).

lated, would lead to the greatest good for the greatest number as if guided by an invisible hand. To the conservatives, the reform doctrines that emerged in the late 1800's were abhorrent concepts that threatened to subvert the most basic values of the American tradition.

During the 1890's, social forces pushed the reform and conservative viewpoints into increasing polarization.[2] From the beginning of the decade on, events moved toward a state of social tension and crisis. By the late 1880's, recovery from the recession that began in 1883 was complete. 1888 and 1889 were years of relative prosperity. By 1892, however, the pressure on the political system by advocates of reform had again become very intense:

> In that year [1892] the newly founded Populist party, catalyzing the rising agrarian unrest, prepared to challenge the major parties in the fall elections. The platform of the party . . . served as a rallying point for much of the protest and reformist movement. In addition to such standard agrarian demands as the free coinage of silver and credit inflation, the platform also demanded government ownership of railroads, telegraph and telephone, a graduated income tax, and the extension of the eight-hour day. The adoption of the platform was followed by a wild demonstration of six thousand people, described by one reporter as "one of the most exciting scenes ever witnessed in a political convention."
>
> Then . . . [just two days later] the widespread labor unrest of the early 1890's erupted violently at the Carnegie steel works in Homestead, Pennsylvania, when strikers of the Amalgamated Association of Iron and Steel Workers fought a pitched battle with three hundred Pinkerton guards.[3]

The result of these events in the early 1890's was "a general hardening of conservative attitudes."[4]

Then followed the panic of 1893 and the beginning of a severe depression "which in the course of the next few years would exacerbate class antagonism in every sphere of social life."[5] As the depression deepened in 1894, the tension between the reformers and the conservatives moved toward a climax. Coxey's "armies" (groups recruited by Jacob S. Coxey from the more than 2,000,000 unemployed in the nation) marched on Washington, receiving enthusiastic welcomes from

---

2. These developments have been carefully chronicled in Paul, *Conservative Crisis*. The discussion that follows relies heavily on Paul's analysis.

3. Paul, *Conservative Crisis*, 75.

4. *Id.*, 76.

5. *Id.*, 82.

the Populist governors of several Midwestern States. To the conservatives, Coxey's armies, like Shays' Rebellion of 1786, appeared as an eruption of the forces of anarchy.

But even Coxey's armies paled in comparison to the threat unleashed by renewed labor militancy. During 1894, over 700,000 workers were out on strike. Most celebrated was the Pullman strike led by Eugene V. Debs.

> And on May 11, 1894 began the famous strike at Pullman, Illinois; with the entrance into the fray on June 26 of the 150,000 men of the American Railway Union, organized for aggressive action and determined to make the strike a major test of labor solidarity, the conflict of the 1890's between capital and labor came to a climax.[6]

As social tension and demands for reform intensified, the conservative backlash intensified as well. The growing conservatism of the mid-1890's can be illustrated by the following quotation from Theodore Roosevelt (an individual often claimed as a hero by the progressive movement and therefore presumably not representative of the far right) regarding William Jennings Bryan and other leaders of the Democratic campaign in the election of 1896.

> I speak with the greatest soberness when I say that the sentiment now animating a large proportion of our people can only be suppressed, as the Commune in Paris was suppressed, by taking ten or a dozen of their leaders out, standing them against a wall, and shooting them dead. I believe it will come to that. These leaders are plotting a social revolution and the subversion of the American Republic.[7]

Gradually at first, but then with gathering momentum, the conservative backlash of the 1890's swept the Supreme Court far to the right. Here is how Paul described the shift:

> In the 1890's the pressures on the Court came from large propertied interests who opposed reform, labor unionism, and economic regulation they could not control. Moderate traditionalists on the bench, misconstruing the social tensions of protest and depression as the coming of majoritarian radicalism, succumbed to these pressures. The Supreme Court (and the judiciary in general) moved to the right, buttressed the ideological rigidities of laissez faire, and carried through a conservative-oriented constitutional revolution.[8]

---

6. *Id.*, 130.
7. H. Pringle, *Theodore Roosevelt* (1931), 114.
8. Paul, *Conservative Crisis*, xiv–xv.

Although the proponents of police power retained substantial strength on the Supreme Court until the 1890's, the tide began to turn inexorably toward judicial enthronement of laissez faire in the 1880's. As late as March 1888, the Court had four members (Waite, Miller, Bradley, and Harlan) who normally voted to uphold economic reform legislation, and only one member (Field) who can be characterized as an extreme conservative on economic issues. By 1896, the situation had exactly reversed, and a solid four-vote conservative bloc (Field, Brewer, Peckham, and Fuller) confronted a liberal wing that had been reduced to one (Harlan).

The first major change occurred when Chief Justice Waite died in March 1888 and was replaced by Melville W. Fuller (1888–1910). Although not as doctrinaire as Field, Brewer, and Peckham, the new Chief Justice was a conservative on economic issues.[9] Shortly thereafter, in January 1890, David Brewer was sworn in to replace the moderate Matthews. Brewer was Field's nephew and, like his uncle, an advocate of laissez faire conservatism.[10] The following exerpts from Brewer's 1891 Yale University commencement address demonstrate his commitment to protecting private property.

> From the time in the earliest records, when Eve took loving possession of even the forbidden apple, the idea of property and the sacredness of the right of its possession have never departed from the race. Whatever dreams may exist of an ideal human nature . . . actual human experience, from the dawn of history to the present hour, declares that the love of acquirement, mingled with the joy of possession, is the real stimulus to human activity. When, among the affirmatives of the Declaration of Independence, it is asserted that the pursuit of happiness is one of the unalienable rights, it is meant that the acquisition, possession and enjoyment of property are matters which human government cannot forbid and which it cannot destroy. . . .
>
> It [the police power] is the refuge of timid judges to escape the obligations of denouncing a wrong, in a case in which some supposed general and public good is the object of legislation. . . . I am here to say to you, in no spirit of obnoxious or unpleasant criticism upon the decision of any tribunal or judge, that the demands of absolute and eternal justice forbid that any private property, legally acquired and legally held, should

---

9. *See, e.g.,* W. King, *Melville Weston Fuller*; 2 Friedman & Israel, *The Justices of the United States*, 1515–23. "In sum, he was a conservative *laissez faire* Justice, less reactionary than some of his brethren, more compassionate than others, but a spokesman for what now seems a far-off and bygone age." *Id.*, 1481.

10. *See supra* p. 74.

be spoliated or destroyed in the interests of public health, morals or welfare without compensation.[11]

Paul suggests that the Fuller and Brewer appointments caused a noticeable shift to the right in the Court's position on economic issues as early as 1890.

> The case [*Chicago, Milwaukee & St. Paul Ry. Co. v. Minnesota*[12]] was also significant in that it was the first indication of how recent changes in personnel might have affected the Court's views. Chief Justice Morrison R. Waite, a staunch defender of the police power, had died in 1888, to be replaced by Melville W. Fuller of Illinois. And in 1889, Justice Stanley Matthews, a moderate conservative of states' rights leaning, had been succeeded by David J. Brewer of Kansas, already known for his refusal to follow the *Munn* case as a United States Circuit Judge. Both Fuller and Brewer . . . were soon to find themselves within the extreme conservative wing on the Court, reinforcing the position that Field had long held alone.[13]

The shift to the right accelerated during the nineteenth century's last decade when the Court lost two of its strongest liberal Justices. In 1890, Miller died. His successor, Henry B. Brown (1891–1906), although by no means an arch-conservative, was neither as dominant nor as liberal as Miller.[14] In 1892, Bradley died. His replacement, George Shiras, Jr. (1892–1903), was a moderate conservative who, to cite one pertinent example, provided the fifth vote to invalidate the income tax in 1895.[15]

After a few additional appointments that did not particularly affect the Bench's economic complexion,[16] the conservative revolution in

---

11. Paul, *Conservative Crisis*, 70–71.

12. 134 U.S. 418 (1890).

13. Paul, *Conservative Crisis*, 42.

14. *See, e.g.*, 2 Friedman & Israel, *The Justices of the United States*, 1553–63, which suggests that although Brown thought of himself as a conservative, he was one of the more moderate members of the extremely conservative Court of the 1890's. "There is no doubt that as a Supreme Court Justice Brown usually took the center position. He was neither a liberal nor a reactionary. . . ." *Id.*, 1557.

15. Shiras has been labelled "middle-of-the-road." 2 Friedman & Israel, *The Justices of the United States*, 1577. However, "[w]hen we observe Shiras' position on national regulatory power, we find him definitely on the right, close to the ultraconservative bloc in annulling or construing narrowly federal reform legislation." *Id.*, 1584.

16. The additional appointments were the following. Justice Woods had died in 1887. His replacement, the conservative Lucius Q.C. Lamar (1888–93), served only five years and was succeeded by Howell Jackson (1893–95). Samuel Blatchford died in 1893 and was succeeded by Edward D. White (1894–1921), who became Chief Justice

Court personnel was completed in 1896, when Rufus W. Peckham
(1896–1909) replaced Howell Jackson. Peckham, the New York judge
who strongly dissented from the lower court's decision in *Budd v. New
York*,[17] was another arch-conservative who moved directly into the
Court's far right wing with Field and Brewer.

With Peckham on board, the Court reached, for the time being, the
extremity of its swing to the right. Table 10 shows the line-up of Justices
after Peckham's arrival.

TABLE 10
Alignment of Justices, 1896

Left	Center	Right
Harlan	White	Field
	Shiras	Brewer
	Brown	Peckham
	Gray	Fuller

Even Harlan, who was quite liberal in civil rights cases, was arguably
only a moderate on purely economic issues. For the conservatives, then,
the mid-1890's were a shining moment with Field, Brewer, Peckham,
and Fuller controlling the Court and writing the doctrines of Social
Darwinism and laissez faire into the nation's fundamental law.

Back in the late 1880's, the economic conservatism that was soon to
be dominant on the Supreme Court can be seen emerging, particularly
in state court decisions holding that efforts to regulate business activity
were illegal deprivations of "liberty of contract"[18] and that strikes by
organized labor were "criminal conspiracies" which courts should enjoin.[19]

---

when Fuller died in 1910. "The judicial whimsy indicated by Justice White's erratic
pattern in these basic substantive due process cases should not obscure the fact that
White tended to vote conservatively, especially as he grew older." 2 Friedman & Israel,
The Justices of the United States, 1645.

17. *See supra* pp. 73–74.

18. The proponents of liberty of contract argued that laissez faire was a blessing to
the poor in that it gave them the opportunity to be self-reliant and to pull themselves
out of their plight without any help from the government. For example, "It [a scrip act]
is a species of sumptuary legislation which has been universally condemned, as an attempt to foist upon the people a paternal government of the most objectionable character, because it assumes that the employer is a knave and the laborer an imbecile."
State v. Goodwill, 33 W. Va. 179 (1889).

19. That the class nature of social conflict in the 1890's was recognized on the Su-

On the Supreme Court, glimmers of the new conservatism were seen as early as 1890, when *Chicago, Milwaukee & St. Paul Ry. Co. v. Minnesota*[20] held unconstitutional a Minnesota rate regulation statute that purported to make rate decisions of the state regulatory commission final and to deny any right of judicial review. The opinion of the Court laid down the crucial doctrine that, *Munn v. Illinois* notwithstanding, the question of reasonable rates was for the Court to determine.[21]

It was 1895, however, that marked the climax of the conservative constitutional revolution of the 1890's.[22] In that year, the Court handed down another trilogy of famous cases comparable in importance and symbolic significance to the 1819 and 1837 trilogies discussed in earlier chapters.

This trilogy began with *United States v. E.C. Knight Co.*,[23] a case that nearly destroyed the ability of the federal government to combat monopoly in the private sector. In 1890, Congress enacted one of the most important pieces of economic reform legislation to that date, the Sherman Act, which gave the Justice Department authority to seek injunctions against monopolies and restraints of trade. The Justice Department thereupon brought suit to force dissolution of the monopolistic sugar trust that controlled over 90 percent of the nation's sugar refining capacity. Speaking through Chief Justice Fuller, the Court held that the action must be dismissed. The Sherman Act, Fuller reasoned, was enacted pursuant to the commerce clause. The suit, however, was directed not at "commerce," that is transportation and sales, but at "manufacturing," a "local" activity reserved by the tenth amendment for exclusive state control. Relief must be denied, the Court concluded, because Congress has no power to regulate local manufacturing. This

---

preme Court is made clear in the following statement by Justice Brown, previously quoted *supra* at p. 7: "The history of civilized society is largely a story of strife between those who have and those who have not." Social conflict, the Justice continued, is largely the result of "the desire of the rich to obtain the labor of the poor at the lowest possible terms, the desire of the poor to obtain the uttermost farthing from the rich." Quoted in Paul, *Conservative Crisis*, 85.

20. 134 U.S. 418 (1890).

21. Just a few years later, the Court first exercised its power to set aside railroad rates established by a state commission. *Reagan v. Farmers' Loan & Trust Co.*, 154 U.S. 362 (1894).

22. "The year 1895 marked the crest for right-wing judicial conservatism." 3 Friedman & Israel, *The Justices of the United States*, 1525. "The Fuller court reached the peak of its commitment to the conservative cause in 1895...." *Id.*, 1485.

23. 156 U.S. 1 (1895).

decision eliminated the United States government's authority to control the conduct of manufacturing corporations.

The second and equally dramatic blow fell later that year when the Court, in *Pollock v. Farmers' Loan & Trust Co.*,[24] held that the Constitution forbids enactment of a graduated income tax. Joseph H. Choate, lead counsel for the opponents of the tax, evoked the spirits of anarchy and communism and prophesied the end of civilization if the tax were allowed to stand.

> The Act . . . is communistic in its purposes and tendencies, and is defended here upon principles as communistic, socialistic—what shall I call them—populistic as ever have been addressed to any political assembly in the world. . . .
>
> I have thought that one of the fundamental objects of all civilized government was the preservation of private property. I have thought that it was the very keystone of the arch upon which all civilized government rests, and that this once abandoned, everything was in danger. . . . According to the doctrines that have been propounded here this morning, even that great fundamental principle has been scattered to the winds.[25]

The Court responded by overturning a century of authority and invalidating the tax. The effect of the decision was to prevent all graduated taxation of income until 1913, when the progressives finally passed the sixteenth amendment explicitly authorizing such taxes.

The third key decision of 1895 was In re *Debs*,[26] which upheld the labor injunctions issued in the Pullman strike of 1894. This ruling, which approved the use of courts as a means of preventing collective action by organized labor, completed the Court's rout of populist programs for economic reform.

> And on May 27, one week after the *Pollock* decision, the Supreme Court handed down its opinion in the *Debs* case, bestowing its official sanction on the new uses of the labor injunction. . . . The judicial developments of the spring of 1895 marked at last the acceptance of that judicial guardianship so determinedly advocated by right-wing conservatism.[27]

Robert H. Jackson, a Supreme Court Justice serving from 1941 to 1954, provided an analysis that highlights the drastic effect of the 1895

---

24. 157 U.S. 429 (1895).
25. *Id.*, 532–34.
26. 158 U.S. 564 (1895).
27. Paul, *Conservative Crisis*, 219.

trilogy on the reform movement.[28] He pointed out that there are three basic ways in which government can redress the balance of power that normally favors the rich against the poor: 1) by redistributing wealth from the rich to the poor through taxes, 2) by regulating activities of the rich, and 3) by encouraging the poor to unite in order to gain bargaining power through numbers. Jackson stated:

> The central problem of democratic government became one of working out a tolerable balance among these forces [industry, finance, agriculture, and labor], of moderating the always threatening power of those whom society permits to own or control its economic resources.... Our history demonstrates that our legislatures saw the answer roughly in this way: *first*, there must be a tax policy, based on ability to pay, sufficient to support social services for those upon whom systematic inequalities bore most harshly—in short, an income tax; *secondly*, there must be regulation of the power of wealth where the premise of competition failed; *thirdly*, those without wealth must be protected in their efforts to organize.[29]

The 1895 trilogy struck directly at each of these fundamental methods of reform activity. *Pollock* denied government the power to impose an income tax. *E.C. Knight* denied government the power to regulate the activities of manufacturing corporations, including the monopolistic trusts. *Debs* denied workers the right to strike in support of their demands. Thus, the 1895 rulings comprised a systematic judicial assault on the methods available to the poor in their quest for economic well-being.

Economic reformers were furious. Justice Brown's *Pollock* dissent illustrates their concerns:

> [The Court's decision] involves nothing less than a surrender of the taxing power to the moneyed class.... Even the spectre of socialism is conjured up to frighten Congress from laying taxes upon people in proportion to their ability to pay them. It is certainly a strange commentary ... that Congress has no power to lay a tax which is one of the main sources of revenue of nearly every civilized State.... I hope it may not prove the first step toward the submergence of the liberties of the people in a sordid despotism of wealth.[30]

Stung, the forces of economic liberalism threw their energy behind the 1896 presidential candidacy of reformer William Jennings Bryan,

---

28. R. Jackson, *The Struggle for Judicial Supremacy* (1941), 39–40.
29. *Id.*
30. 158 U.S. at 695 (on rehearing).

in an effort to carry out a counterrevolution through the electorate. Bryan's platform included measures directed against the Court and its laissez faire policies. However, the electoral effort failed. Bryan was defeated by the conservative William McKinley. The outcome has been described as follows:

> The defeat of Bryan ... was a great victory for American conservatism. ... The judicial triumph of conservatism in the spring of 1895 had been confirmed by the political triumph of 1896. The conservative crisis of the 1890's was over.[31]

In the aftermath of its 1895 conservative revolution, the Court continued in an activist manner to fulfill its newly acquired role as judicial censor of economic reform legislation.[32] Substantive due process—the centerpiece of constitutional economic conservatism—took on its definitive form in the 1890's. The 1897 case, *Allgeyer v. Louisiana*,[33] was the first to employ the fully mature substantive due process/liberty of contract doctrine to nullify a state economic statute.[34]

According to this doctrine, socio-economic legislation that unreasonably restricts the liberty of individuals and corporations to make contracts and use their property as they see fit denies the due process required by the Constitution's fifth and fourteenth amendments. This same theory had been rejected, over Justice Field's dissent, in the 1873 *Slaughter-House Cases* on the ground that "due process" is concerned only with procedural regularity and not with the reasonableness of government action.[35] In the conservative climate of the 1890's, the Court reversed itself and adopted Field's proposition that the due process clauses impose substantive restraints on economic legislation.[36] During the remainder of its second conservative era, the Court used

---

31. Paul, *Conservative Crisis*, 226.

32. The conservatism of the Court in the 1890's was not limited to the area of economic reform legislation. In the race relations area, for example, the Court continued its reactionary course by approving the "separate but equal" formula that nullified the equal protection clause and ratified the Jim Crow system of legally sanctioned segregation. *E.g., Plessy v. Ferguson*, 163 U.S. 537 (1896). Similarly, the Court was very conservative in criminal procedure cases.

33. 165 U.S. 578 (1897).

34. The statute concerned out-of-State insurance sales.

35. *See supra* p. 67.

36. *Cf. Smyth v. Ames*, 169 U.S. 466 (1898), another well known conservative decision holding that due process requires state railroad commissions to set rates high enough to allow a fair return on a fair valuation of the railroads' property, as determined according to a formula established by the Court itself.

this interpretation of due process to strike down child labor laws, minimum wage/maximum hour regulations, legislation outlawing anti-labor "yellow dog" contracts, rate regulation of railroads and other corporate entities, as well as several major New Deal reforms.

While waging its war against economic reform, the Fuller Court availed itself of a number of powerful constitutional weapons in addition to substantive due process. State economic reform laws were repeatedly invalidated on the ground that they unreasonably burdened interstate commerce and thus violated the dormant commerce clause. Out of whole cloth, the Court invented the rule, later repudiated, that the Constitution's tenth amendment created a system of "dual federalism" in which enormous areas of economic activity, including production (manufacturing, mining, and agriculture), were exclusively reserved for the States and hence immune from federal legislation. The tenth amendment/dual federalism theory was also used to restrict other federal legislative powers such as the prerogatives to tax and spend. Other constitutional provisions used to restrain economic reforms included the contract clause and the equal protection clause.

However, although the dominant theme of the 1890–1905 period of Supreme Court history was economic conservatism, it would be mistaken to conclude that liberal decisions were entirely absent from the Justices' holdings. On the contrary, just as the Taney Court had its conservative side, the Fuller Court had a liberal side too. Perhaps the most important expression of that liberalism was the emergence of a new, broad interpretation of the commerce power, authorizing federal "police power" regulation of matters previously relegated to the States.

The leading case in this line was *Champion v. Ames*,[37] which held that congressional authority "to regulate commerce . . . among the several States" included the power to exclude lottery tickets from interstate commerce. The power to exclude was considered plenary, and could be exercised to destroy commerce in undesired commodities as well as to protect commerce in desired commodities.

Similarly, many state economic reform laws survived the test of constitutionality before the Court during this period. Indeed, some conservatives complained that the Court was not doing enough to stem the tide of socialism. Their concern was, for practical purposes, without cause. On the Fuller Court, liberalism was, without question, subordinate to the primary theme of conservative constitutional activism.

---

37. 188 U.S. 321 (1903).

As the nineteenth century drew to a close, the hard line endorsed by the Court majority gradually softened. The severe depression that descended in 1893 eased in late 1897. By the following year, recovery was well underway and the start of a long period of relatively stable prosperity (1898–1914) was at hand. This brought a lessening of the social unrest that had, in turn, prompted the conservative backlash. "With the passing of the social and economic tensions of the mid-1890's the Court tended toward moderation in the use of its expanded powers."[38]

In addition, a series of relatively liberal appointments pushed the Bench into a more moderate posture. In 1897, the conservative Field retired. He was replaced by Joseph McKenna (1898–1925), who had been rather conservative prior to his judicial career, developed into a moderate, and then moved back to the right late in his tenure.[39] In 1902, the moderate Horace Gray was succeeded by one of the giants of Supreme Court history, Oliver Wendell Holmes, Jr. (1902–32), a basically conservative individual who became a leading liberal Justice due to his deep commitment to judicial restraint.[40] The next year, the moderate conservative Shiras was replaced by William R. Day (1903–22), a moderate.[41] Table 11 shows the closely balanced line-up after those three appointments.

TABLE 11
Alignment of Justices, 1903–06

Left	Center	Right
Harlan	White	Brewer
Holmes	Day	Peckham
	Brown	Fuller
	McKenna	

Despite the gradual liberalization of Court personnel and public

---

38. 3 Friedman & Israel, *The Justices of the United States*, 1528.

39. M. McDevitt, *Joseph McKenna, passim* (1946); 3 Friedman & Israel, *The Justices of the United States*, 1719–36.

40. Holmes is probably the second most famous and admired Justice in the Court's history, ranking only behind John Marshall. Holmes played a major role in the Court's liberal wing for many years and will be mentioned frequently in later pages.

41. "To his credit, Day, in recognizing many of the vast social changes, adjusted his legal philosophy and became a moderate liberal in terms of favoring the extension of federal powers. Except for his stubborn reliance on Melville Fuller's odd definition of commerce, Justice Day generally cast his vote on the side of the twentieth century." 3 Friedman & Israel, *The Justices of the United States*, 1788.

opinion in the nation at large, the Court's first age of laissez faire continued at least until 1905, when the most notorious substantive due process decision of all, *Lochner v. New York*,[42] came down. At issue was a New York statute limiting the working day of bakery employees to ten hours. For years, minimum wage/maximum hour legislation had been one of the most basic and consistent demands of the economic reform movement. At the same time, conservatives considered the question of wages and hours to be at the heart of the "liberty of contract" granted exemption from governmental regulation.

In *Lochner*, the Court, by a narrow 5–4 margin, held the maximum hour statute to be an unconstitutional infringement of liberty of contract. The majority included, of course, the "three archconservatives,"[43] Peckham, who wrote the opinion, Brewer, and Fuller. Harlan, Holmes, Day, and White dissented. Had it not been for the defection of McKenna, the liberals would have prevailed. The *Lochner* case shows that the forces of laissez faire were still in control as late as 1905 but that the margin of dominance was growing thin.

---

42. 198 U.S. 45 (1905).
43. 3 Friedman & Israel, *The Justices of the United States*, 1533.

9
The Not Quite Progressive Era (1906–1920)[1]

In the face of entrenched conservatism on the Supreme Court, the popular forces that presented the rich with formidable challenges during the late 1800's did not fold their tents and disappear into the night. On the contrary, the reformers swallowed hard and then continued their struggle in the tradition of the Grangers, Populists, labor organizers, free silver inflationists, and suffragettes who were their political ancestors.

Early in the 1900's, the reform movement began to recover from the judicial setbacks of the 1890's and to register significant gains once again. After a short while, a coalition operating under the name of progressivism attained political ascendancy first within key state governments and then on a national scale. As with Jeffersonianism, however, progressivism never succeeded in gaining control of the Supreme Court. Rather the coalition's achievements were greatest in the executive and legislative branches.

The progressives took control of the Democratic Party in 1896. From then until 1911, the party was for the most part dominated by "the Great Commoner," William Jennings Bryan, a thoroughgoing re-

---

1. Helpful sources for this period include H. Croly, *The Promise of American Life* (1963); A. Link, *Woodrow Wilson and the Progressive Era* (1954); A. Mason, *Brandeis, A Free Man's Life* (1946); H. Pringle, *Theodore Roosevelt* (1931); A. Schlesinger, *The Crisis of the Old Order* (1957).

As previously indicated, designation of the year 1906 as the start of the Court's "not quite progressive" era is somewhat arbitrary. *See supra* note 36, chapter 7. Clearly the Court moved from a reactionary posture in the 1890's to a more liberal posture in the years before and after 1910, but no clear cut boundary exists between the two periods. A case can be made for selecting the year 1910, when Charles Evans Hughes was seated, as the start of the "liberal interlude." Pfeffer, *This Honorable Court*, 250–53. The choice of 1906 as the starting point is based primarily on the seating of William H. Moody, which brought the liberal wing back to parity with the conservative wing, and on the fact that liberal decisions began to appear in greater numbers in the 1906–10 period. Note also that 1906 was the year in which Charles Evans Hughes was elected Governor of New York on a reform platform.

former and champion of the poor. Bryan, a former Nebraska congress-man and prominent spokesman for the 1894 income tax held uncon-stitutional in *Pollock*, was first nominated for the presidency by the Democrats in 1896 after his famous "You shall not crucify mankind upon a cross of gold" speech. Bryan was also the Democratic presiden-tial candidate in 1900 and 1908. During this period (from 1896 to 1911), however, the Democrats were unable to win a presidential elec-tion.

The impulse for reform was so strong that it also began to make in-roads within the Republican Party, which, since the 1870's, had been dominated by the interests of wealth and conservativism. To be sure, the Republicans continued to have stalwart conservative leaders such as President McKinley and Nelson Aldrich, the dominant voice of the Sen-ate. But by the turn of the century progressive Republican "insurgents" were making their presence felt. In 1900, for example, Robert M. La Follette was elected Governor of Wisconsin and promptly turned the State into a "laboratory of democracy."[2]

The Republican progressives received a major boost when McKinley was assassinated in 1901 and succeeded by Theodore Roosevelt, the fairweather reformer whose presidency lasted until 1909. Roosevelt's "Square Deal" programs included significant efforts to curb the ex-cesses of the "malefactors of great wealth." Among his most publicized measures were stiff enforcement of antitrust laws ("trust busting") and a campaign for the conservation of natural resources. His tenure also saw the enactment of the Pure Food and Drug Act, the Federal Employ-ers' Liability Act, the Hepburn Act, which restored the ICC's power to set railroad rates, and a variety of other economic reform statutes.

Roosevelt additionally made three rather liberal appointments to the Supreme Court. Following his success in getting the liberal Holmes and the moderate Day seated on the Bench,[3] he then selected his close friend and advisor William H. Moody (1906–10)[4] to succeed the moderate Brown. Said one commentator: "Moody's legal approach was careful

---

2. C. Sellers & H. May, *A Synopsis of American History* (1963), 284.

3. *See supra* p. 88.

4. *See* 3 Friedman & Israel, *The Justices of the United States*, 1801–21. While in the House of Representatives (1895–1902), Moody played a major role in pushing the Hepburn Act through Congress restoring the ICC's rate-setting powers which had been stripped by the Court. He was a trust-buster who also held "advanced" pro-labor views. At the time of his appointment, he was criticized as "too radical." *Id.*, 1815.

and cautious but distinctly progressive in a liberal nationalistic sense."[5]

Table 12 shows the line-up on the Court from Moody's appointment until 1909.

TABLE 12
Alignment of Justices, 1906–09

Left	Center	Right
Harlan	Day	Brewer
Holmes	White	Peckham
Moody	McKenna	Fuller

Clearly, judicial liberalism had enjoyed a resurgence. On economic issues the Court was closely balanced and no faction was numerically strong enough to claim complete control. But a case can be made that Moody's appointment gave the liberals at least a slight edge for the first time since the early 1890's.

A well known decision indicative of the increased liberalism of the "Teddy Roosevelt Court" was *Muller v. Oregon*.[6] At issue was an Oregon statute prohibiting employment of women more than ten hours a day in factories and laundries. Muller had been convicted of working his women laundry employees in excess of this limit. He appealed claiming the statute unreasonably interfered with his liberty of contract. The statute plainly touched upon what was then regarded as the core of liberty of contract, hours of employment. In 1905, *Lochner v. New York*[7] had held unconstitutional a ten-hour work day statute for men and made it clear that the Court was prepared to nullify wage and hour legislation it found unreasonable.

In order to rebut the claim that the Oregon statute comprised an unreasonable interference with the employer's liberty, Louis Dembitz Brandeis, the "people's lawyer" and later a Supreme Court Justice, submitted his landmark "Brandeis brief," a singular compilation that amassed the available sociological data underscoring the need for protective maximum hour legislation. Brandeis' reliance on empirical studies was a tactic new to the annals of judicial advocacy and introduced a helpful element of reality into the Court's analysis of rich-poor

5. *Id.*, 1819.
6. 208 U.S. 412 (1908).
7. 198 U.S. 45 (1905). *See supra* p. 89.

issues. In *Muller*, it played a major role in persuading the Justices to uphold the Oregon statute unanimously.

Such victories for economic liberalism were, however, matched during this period by equally impressive wins for the conservatives. In *Adair v. United States*,[8] for example, a federal statute prohibiting anti-labor yellow dog contracts was held unconstitutional.[9] That same year, in *Loewe v. Lawlor*,[10] the Court held labor unions to be subject to the Sherman Act, the 1890 statute prohibiting restraints of trade, and affirmed a treble damage award against representatives of the United Hatters of North America for engaging in a boycott found to be illegal.

A decision perfectly illustrating the Court's conservative-liberal split was the *First Employers' Liability Cases*,[11] which held the 1906 Federal Employers' Liability Act unconstitutional because it purported to cover employees not involved in interstate commerce and therefore exceeded the power of Congress under the commerce clause. Justice White wrote the opinion for the five-vote majority that included the conservatives Brewer, Peckham, and Fuller, and the moderate Day. The Court's entire liberal wing dissented.

Against this background of a closely balanced Supreme Court which supplied progressives with a few tangible judicial gains without seriously jeopardizing the predominant position of entrenched conservative power, Roosevelt made a major mistake from the progressive point of view. While refusing all entreaties to seek a third presidential term, he placed his considerable influence solidly in support of William Howard Taft's bid for the nomination. Taft was a conservative at heart, but in the 1908 election year he was temporarily caught in the grip of a progressive outlook. Professor Link described Roosevelt's failure to perceive Taft's true political nature as follows:

> His one great mistake, and it was an error of personal judgment, was in choosing William Howard Taft to succeed him. If Roosevelt had selected Charles Evans Hughes, the brilliant, crusading, and independent Governor of New York, the future history of the United States might have been considerably different.[12]

---

8. 208 U.S. 161 (1908).

9. A yellow dog cotract is an employment contract containing an agreement by the employee not to join a union.

10. 208 U.S. 274 (1908) (the so-called Danbury Hatters' case).

11. 207 U.S. 463 (1908).

12. Link, *Woodrow Wilson and the Progressive Era*, 3.

After his election, Taft lost little time in aligning himself with the Republican Party's conservative Old Guard and against its progressive insurgents. In the 1910 off-year election, for example, he helped orchestrate a general attempt to defeat Midwest progressive Republicans. To quote Link again:

> In order to prevent the disruption of the Republican Party, Taft had to facilitate the shift in party control from Old Guard to the insurgents. Instead of boldly doing this, he vacillated at first, finally aligned himself with the reactionaries, and so completely alienated the progressives that a rupture was inevitable.[13]

Ironically, the chance to reduce the influence of laissez faire on the Supreme Court and inaugurate a new phase of economic liberalism came in 1909 and 1910 when all three of the Bench's arch-conservatives, Brewer, Peckham, and Fuller, died. With the progressive movement then gaining momentum on a national scale, had Taft remained in the mold that sparked so much enthusiasm on his predecessor's part, the liberals could easily have picked up the extra votes needed to assure their primacy on the Court.[14] At this time, however, Roosevelt's "mistake" made itself felt, for precisely at this time Taft moved sharply to the right politically.

Because of Moody's 1910 retirement and Harlan's 1911 death, Taft had five seats to fill and thus could have created a 7–2 progressive majority if he had wished. Instead, his choices were four moderates and conservatives, Horace Lurton (1910–14), Willis Van Devanter (1911–37), Joseph Lamar (1911–16), and Mahlon Pitney (1912–22), and only one progressive, Charles Evans Hughes (1910–16).[15] As a result, the liberal bloc was actually reduced from three to two.

---

13. *Id.*

14. Actually, if McKenna, who was then in his more liberal middle period is counted as an economic liberal, for a brief time after the appointment of Charles Evans Hughes (1910–16), the Court arguably had a five-vote liberal majority (Harlan, Holmes, Hughes, Moody, and McKenna). Moody, however, had already become partially disabled by the rheumatism that forced his retirement in 1910 and left him crippled, and Harlan died within the year. So the moment was fleeting.

15. Horace Lurton was a jurist of "ingrained conservatism" who had a "general conservative approach" to legal questions. 3 Friedman & Israel, *The Justices of the United States*, 1855. At the time of his appointment, protests were raised because of Lurton's alleged "favoritism" toward corporations and property rights, and Samuel Gompers labelled him a "narrow conservative." *Id.*, 1888. During his brief term on the Court, Lurton was a moderate.

Willis Van Devanter was a conservative who, after a somewhat moderate first few

Table 13 shows the line-up on the Court after Taft's five appointees were seated.

TABLE 13
Alignment of Justices, 1911–14

Left	Center	Right
Holmes	White	Van Devan-
Hughes	Lurton	ter
	Pitney	Lamar
	Day	
	McKenna	

Taft's appointments did not appreciably alter the somewhat more liberal viewpoints that had characterized the Court since 1906. A combination of factors contributed to the continuity of this balance. First, the new conservatives were far less extreme in their thinking than men like Field, Brewer, and Peckham. Second the progressive Charles Evans Hughes seems to have exerted an influence on his peers in excess of his one vote in nine. Third, and most important, the Court was affected by the increasingly progressive climate of public opinion throughout the nation.

In 1910, the progressive movement achieved its greatest political victories to date. Within the Republican Party, the struggle between progressives and conservatives reached a climax in the spring of that year. When Taft aligned himself with the conservatives, the progressives

---

years, became a stalwart of the Court's right wing. "[H]e was the most intractable of the reactionary justices of the 1930's." *Id.*, 1952. Harlan Fiske Stone later described him as "the commander-in-chief of the judicial reaction." *Id.*

Joseph R. Lamar was a "cautious, temperate, and conservative" Justice who "accepted the predominant conservative ideas of his era." *Id.*, 1988.

Mahlon Pitney was a "conservative of the Taft stripe." A. Mason, *The Supreme Court from Taft to Warren* (1958), 54. His appointment was opposed by the progressives. On the Court, he took a strongly anti-labor, anti-civil liberties position and helped fulfill "Taft's expectations... [that] the Court would act as the great bulwark against radical innovation." 3 Friedman & Israel, *The Justices of the United States*, 2001.

Charles Evans Hughes, on the other hand, was "one of the outstanding liberal members of the Court during his initial period of service." *Id.*, 1901. Later in his career, Hughes' "essentially conservative cast of mind" pushed him into a more moderate position." *Id.*, 1914.

turned to the idea of a third party under the leadership of Theodore Roosevelt.

The net result of Taft's shift to the right and the ensuing split in Republican ranks was a Democratic victory in the 1910 off-year elections. For the first time since 1892, Democrats took control of the House of Representatives. Moreover, progressive candidates swept into power in a number of key States. For example, Woodrow Wilson captured New Jersey's governorship and Hiram Johnson overthrew the dominance of the Southern Pacific to become California's governor. Both Wilson and Johnson inaugurated economic reform programs within their respective States.

Progressive ascendancy in the federal government came with the election of 1912. By then, the split within the Republican Party had become irreconcilable. When the pro-Taft forces steamrollered the Republican nominating convention, Theodore Roosevelt and his faction walked out. On August 6, 1912, the Progressive, or Bull Moose, Party was formed. The new party selected as its presidential candidate Theodore Roosevelt, who was at this point an enthusiastic progressive.

Enthusiasm notwithstanding, Taft and Roosevelt split the Republican vote in the November election, allowing Woodrow Wilson to win a plurality victory. At the same time, the Democrats retained their control of the House and captured the Senate as well. Wilson, personally an interesting mix of conservatism and progressivism, had run on a strongly progressive platform. Thus, the election amounted to a major victory for the advocates of economic reform.[16]

Wilson's 1913 inauguration was followed by a burst of legislation in keeping with his progressive platform. In rapid succession, statutes were passed imposing a graduated income tax,[17] reducing the protective tariffs that had sheltered big business for years, and regulating the banking system, then known as the "money trust," that had been dominated by the House of Morgan, the Rockefeller Group (including Kuhn, Loeb & Co.), and other financial powers. Simultaneously, progressive measures continued to flow out of state legislatures as well.

---

16. The progressive mood within the country was so strong that both progressives, Wilson and Roosevelt, ran well ahead of the conservative Taft. In fact, the real contest was between the Democrats and the Progressives, with the Republicans pretty much conceding long before the election.

17. The sixteenth amendment had been ratified in 1913, removing the obstacle created by the *Pollock* case.

Naturally, the progressive economic reforms were promptly challenged in the courts. "The hot controversy of the day," legal historian Merlo J. Pusey has stated, "was over the extent to which 'freedom of contract' restrained the states from passing social legislation."[18] In a substantial number of these challenges, the advocates of social and economic reform prevailed. Thus, to cite two instances, the Court unanimously upheld statutes imposing a maximum 10-hour day for women in *Riley v. Massachusetts*[19] and an 8-hour day, 48-hour week for women in *Miller v. Wilson*.[20] The Bench's relative tolerance for progressive legislation was also illustrated by Justice Hughes' majority opinion in *Chicago, B.&O. Ry. Co. v. McGuire*[21] upholding a state law that outlawed employment contracts requiring employees to waive their right to sue for damages caused by industrial accidents. Hughes wrote:

> Freedom of contract is a qualified and not an absolute right. There is no absolute freedom to do as one wills or contract as one chooses. The guaranty of liberty does not withdraw from legislative supervision that wide department of activity which consists of the making of contracts or deny to government the power to provide restrictive safeguards. Liberty implies the absence of arbitrary restraint, not immunity from reasonable regulations and prohibitions in the interests of the community.[22]

The Court's conservative wing continued, however, to assert itself at crucial moments. Perhaps the most striking example of the remaining power of laissez faire concepts among the Justices was *Coppage v. Kansas*,[23] which struck down a state statute outlawing yellow dog contracts, thus making the doctrine of *Adair v. United States* applicable to state as well as federal legislation.[24]

In 1916, Justice Hughes resigned from the Court to become the Republican presidential candidate. The Wilson administration, after a relatively conservative period during 1914 and 1915, responded to Hughes' challenge with a second burst of progressive legislation. Statutes were enacted establishing a workers' compensation system, prohibiting the interstate transportation of goods produced by child labor,

---

18. M. Pusey, *Charles Evans Hughes* (1961), 310.
19. 232 U.S. 671 (1914).
20. 236 U.S. 373 (1915).
21. 219 U.S. 549 (1911).
22. *Id.*, 567.
23. 236 U.S. 1 (1915).
24. *Cf. supra* note 8, chapter 9, and accompanying text.

and providing guaranteed loans for farmers and increased self-government for the Philippine Islands. By the close of 1916, the Wilsonian Democrats had transformed essentially their entire 1912 platform into law.[25]

What was the Supreme Court's reaction to this unprecedented wave of reform activity? There can be little doubt that much of the Wilsonian legislative program would have been declared unconstitutional by the Supreme Court of the 1890's. By 1916, however, new appointments had produced a Court whose members were much more flexible regarding what economic regulations were constitutionally permissible. Nevertheless, despite the Court's liberalization, the power of the conservatives was not definitively broken, and the judicial doctrines of laissez faire continued to pose a challenge to economic reform programs.

Although Wilson made only three Supreme Court appointments during his two-term presidency, he had the opportunity to create a five-vote progressive majority on the Bench if all of his nominees had been progressives. He irrevocably lost his chance, however, when he selected James C. McReynolds (1914–41) to replace Horace Lurton. McReynolds, who had achieved a reputation as a liberal because of his work on Justice Department antitrust litigation, turned out to be one of the most conservative Justices ever to sit on the highest Court.[26]

From the perspective of progressivism, Wilson did much better with his next two nominations. In 1916, Hughes resigned and Lamar died. Wilson, at the time, was in a mood of advanced domestic progressivism and selected two liberals to fill the openings. The first was Louis Dembitz Brandeis (1916–38), "the first thoroughgoing progressive ever to be appointed to the Supreme Court."[27] The second was John H. Clarke (1916–22), who was "known for his liberal views" and who wrote to Brandeis, "I am looking forward with unusual confidence to pleasant association with you because of what I suppose is something

---

25. Link, *Woodrow Wilson and the Progressive Era*, 223 *et seq.*

26. A strong case can be made for the proposition that McReynolds is number one in the ranks of reactionary Supreme Court Justices, ahead of even Field, Brewer, and the early Federalists. McReynolds was "the Court's staunchest defender of due process in protecting the rights of businessmen." 3 Friedman & Israel, *The Justices of the United States*, 2030. "Of the four conservative Justices famous for their opposition to Franklin Roosevelt's New Deal, James Clark McReynolds was probably the most reactionary and easily the most tenacious." *Id.*, 2023.

27. Mason, *Brandeis, A Free Man's Life*, 514. In addition to Mason's biography, an excellent source on Brandeis is B. Murphy, *The Brandeis/Frankfurter Connection* (1982).

of a community point of view between us."[28] Wilson clearly hoped Brandeis and Clarke would combat the anti-progressive views that still remained on the Court. A few years later Wilson wrote:

> Like thousands of other liberals throughout the country, I have been counting on the influence of you and Justice Brandeis to restrain the Court in some measure from the extreme reactionary course which it seems inclined to follow.[29]

Table 14 shows the Court's balance of power after the seating of Brandeis and Clarke in 1916.

TABLE 14
Alignment of Justices, 1916–20

Left	Center	Right
Brandeis	White	McReynolds
Holmes	Pitney	Van Devan-
Clarke	Day	ter
McKenna[30]		

At this juncture, the effect of Wilson's McReynolds appointment became clear. Aligning himself with Taft's two remaining appointees, Van Devanter and Pitney, and the moderates, White and Day, McReynolds deprived progressivism of the fifth vote needed to gain control of the Bench. As a result, the dominance of laissez faire remained unbroken.

Hammer v. Dagenhart[31] vividly illustrates the inability of the Court's progressive plurality to bring about an era of judicial liberalism. For many years, one of the reform movement's most consistent demands had been the abolition of child labor, a practice which forced young children of indigent parents to work long hours under terrible conditions. The advocates of laissez faire resisted these demands on the

28. *Id.*, 513. It has been speculated that Brandeis, who had been Wilson's intimate friend and advisor for years, recommended the appointment of Clarke. Justice Clarke was "fairly far to the left within the limits of sound progressivism, and was prepared to back up a broad extension of state and national power." 3 Friedman & Israel, *The Justices of the United States*, 2081. Clarke also showed "particular generosity toward labor." *Id.*, 2083. At the time of his resignation in 1922, the New York Globe wrote, "He is a liberal among conservatives, and he was needed." *Id.*, 2085.

29. Jackson, *The Struggle for Judicial Supremacy*, 186.

30. This was McKenna's most liberal period. Even so, a strong case can be made for listing him as a moderate rather than a liberal on economic issues.

31. 247 U.S. 251 (1918).

ground that such legislation would be paternalistic and would interfere with liberty of contract.

In 1916, the Wilson administration finally succeeded in passing a federal statute prohibiting the interstate shipment of goods manufactured by child labor. The legislation was quickly challenged. When it arrived before the Supreme Court in *Hammer*, the law was declared unconstitutional by a 5–4 vote. Writing for the majority, Justice Day, in the best tradition of laissez faire conservatism, concluded that the real purpose of the statute was to regulate manufacturing and that the Constitution's commerce clause did not give Congress the power to regulate manufacturing as opposed to transportation. Holmes, Brandeis, Clarke, and McKenna dissented futilely.[32]

Since the concurrence of only one of the Bench's three moderate Justices was needed to give the progressives a majority in any case, the progressives continued to enjoy occasional triumphs. A leading example is *Bunting v. Oregon*,[33] which, without mentioning it, overruled the 1905 *Lochner* decision and upheld a general 10-hour day law.[34] McKenna, who had provided the fifth vote for the conservatives in *Lochner*, recanted, joined the progressives, and wrote the majority opinion upholding the statute. Holmes, Clarke, Day, and Pitney were in the majority. Brandeis did not participate because he had been involved in the litigation before joining the Court.[35]

But even these minor progressive victories proved short-lived. For, after almost 15 years of rulings that dispensed substantial gains and losses to progressives and conservatives alike, the prevailing mood of the Court's second conservative era was about to reassert itself, and laissez faire was soon to hold sway once again.

---

32. Other illustrative conservative victories included *Hitchman Coal & Coke Co. v. Mitchell*, 245 U.S. 229 (1918), which upheld injunctions restraining unions from soliciting employees who had signed yellow dog contracts, and *Adams v. Tanner*, 244 U.S. 590 (1917), which held unconstitutional a state law prohibiting employment agency fees.

33. 243 U.S. 426 (1917).

34. *Cf. Wilson v. New*, 243 U.S. 332 (1917), which upheld the Adamson Act's minimum wage and maximum hour provisions covering employees of interstate carriers.

35. After his Court appointment, Brandeis handed the *Bunting* litigation off to his Harvard protege, Professor Felix Frankfurter, who filed a Brandeis Brief on the *Muller* model.

10

The Second Age of Laissez Faire (1921–1937)[1]

A. The 1920's and the Taft Court[2]

In 1920 the Supreme Court was still what Marshall had conceived it to be—the protector and guardian of property. And that was to be its role during the decade in which William Howard Taft was Chief Justice.[3]

The 1920 presidential election was a national referendum in which the voters overwhelmingly rejected progressive government. The nation was tired of reform politics. A record seven million vote landslide in favor of the conservative Republican Warren G. Harding resoundingly demonstrated that the nation wanted to return to "business as usual." The federal government, having grown fat and powerful during World War I, was to be cut back and the business of the nation put into the hands of the free enterprise system.

Former President William Howard Taft, a fervent Harding supporter, worked industriously during the 1920 presidential campaign to make the Supreme Court a major election issue. Taft knew the Court would probably have at least four vacancies in the early 1920's and its future political posture would depend on whether conservatives or liberals got those seats.

Of all Taft's deeds during his presidency, he was perhaps proudest of his conservative appointments to the Court. He was also keenly aware of the manner in which these Justices had used their judicial prerogatives to protect propertied interests against the proponents of progressive reform.[4] Now that his appointees were about to leave the Bench,

---

1. Useful sources concerning this period include R. Jackson, *The Struggle for Judicial Supremacy* (1941); A. Mason, *The Supreme Court From Taft to Warren* (1958); A. Schlesinger, *The Crisis of the Old Order* (1957).
2. *See* Galloway, *The Taft Court (1921–1929)*, 25 Santa Clara L. Rev. 1 (1985).
3. Pfeffer, *This Honorable Court*, 269.
4. Taft's biographer stated, "Above all other things he was proudest of the fact that

Taft was determined to secure replacements who would carry on the conservative tradition and maintain the judiciary as the final bulwark in the defense of property.[5] Here is Taft's most famous statement on this issue during the campaign:

> Mr. Wilson is in favor of a latitudinarian construction of the Constitution of the United States to weaken the protection it should afford against socialistic raids upon property rights.... He has made three appointments to the Supreme Court. He is understood to be greatly disappointed in the attitude of the first of these [McReynolds] upon such questions. The other two [Brandeis and Clarke] represent a new school of constitutional construction, which if allowed to prevail, will greatly impair our fundamental law. Four of the incumbent Justices are beyond the retiring age of seventy, and the next President will probably be called upon to appoint their successors. There is no greater domestic issue in this election than the maintenance of the Supreme Court as the bulwark to enforce the guaranty that no man shall be deprived of his property without the due process of law.[6]

The 1920 Harding landslide gave Taft exactly what he wanted. In the years following Harding's inauguration, vacancies on the Court came swiftly and the empty seats were filled exclusively by conservatives. The first of these was Taft himself (1921–30),[7] who replaced the deceased Chief Justice White, a moderate conservative. Taft's attitude toward organized labor, around which major issues frequently arose, is illustrative of his stern attitude toward the poor in general. On the subject of labor, in a 1922 letter to his brother, he wrote:

> The only class which is distinctly arrayed against the Court is a class that does not like the courts at any rate, and that is organized labor. That faction we have to hit every little while, because they are continually vi-

---

six of the nine members of the Supreme Court bore his commission. 'And I have said to them,' Taft chuckled, 'Damn you, if any of you die, I'll disown you.' " 2 H. Pringle, *The Life and Times of William Howard Taft* (1939), 854.

5. On the side, Taft may also have hoped he would be one of the conservatives chosen if Harding was elected. As it turned out, he was.

6. Mason, *The Supreme Court From Taft to Warren*, 40.

7. "Taft was a thoroughgoing Social Darwinist, stubborn defender of the *status quo*, apologist for economic privilege, inveterate critic of social democracy—the gigantic symbol of stand-pattism." 3 Friedman & Israel, *The Justices of the United States*, 2104. "His enduring aim ... [was] to safeguard private property. Courts were [in Taft's opinion] America's primary reliance for preserving this bulwark of civilization." *Id.*, 2103.

olating the law and depending on threats and violence to accomplish their purpose.[8]

In 1922, Clarke retired and Harding appointed his own 1920 campaign manager, George Sutherland (1922–38), to replace him. Sutherland, a conservative Republican from Utah, "had served in the Senate from 1905 to 1917, where he consistently opposed the progressive policies of Roosevelt and Wilson."[9] He later became the intellectual spokesman for the four-vote conservative bloc of the 1930's. The Clarke-Sutherland succession marked a substantial shift to the right, since it represented the loss of a liberal as well as the addition of a conservative. That same year, the moderate Day retired. His seat was filled by Pierce Butler (1923–39), a Minnesota railroad attorney and an extreme economic conservative.[10] Finally, in 1923, the moderate conservative Pitney retired and was succeeded by Edward Sanford (1923–30), another moderate conservative.

Thus, after Harding reshaped the Court, the majority Justices were as Taft had hoped: extremely conservative on economic issues and ready to strike down any more "socialistic raids" on property rights. For the first time since the pre-Jacksonian period, the Bench had six tried-and-true conservatives. The liberal wing was reduced to practical impotence, as Table 15 shows.

TABLE 15
Alignment of Justices, 1923–25

Left	Center	Right
Brandeis	McKenna	McReynolds
Holmes		Butler
		Sutherland
		Van Devan-
		ter
		Taft
		Sanford

With regard to this alignment, legal historian Alpheus Thomas Mason stated:

---

8. Pfeffer, *This Honorable Court*, 274.

9. *Id.*, 271.

10. "Butler's decisions throughout his years on the Court reveal an almost unrelenting conservatism." 3 Friedman & Israel, *The Justices of the United States*, 2187. "Butler was among the most rigid of the justices who rejected New Deal legislation. His philosophy was that of laissez faire. . . . " *Id.*, 2190.

As Taft had foreseen, reconstitution of the supreme bench quickly followed on the heels of Harding's election. By 1923 four of the nine Justices—George Sutherland, Pierce Butler, Edward Sanford and Taft himself as Chief Justice—had been appointed by the Republican President. With Willis Van Devanter, James McReynolds, and the infirm Joseph McKenna...these four judges—all staunchly conservative—heightened the rigidities of constitutional interpretation. The genial Chief Justice, described by his biographer as "conservative, if not reactionary," had now realized his ambition to preside over a court that could be counted on to quell any "socialistic raids on property rights." Soon after his appointment the Chief Justice (consistent with his view in shaping the law) announced at a conference of the Justices that he "had been appointed to reverse a few decisions" and, with his famous chuckle, added, "I looked right at old Holmes when I said it."[11]

Harding's fulfillment of Taft's aspirations started the Court's second age of laissez faire conservatism. Once again, the majority assumed the task of "censoring" economic legislation and nullifying legislative efforts to regulate the operation of the free enterprise system.[12]

The case which, above all others, symbolizes this renewed surge of judicial conservatism is *Adkins v. Children's Hospital*.[13] At issue was the constitutionality of a minimum wage statute for women and children, exactly the type of legislation that had long been one of the most fundamental progressive demands. In deciding *Adkins*, the Court turned the clock back to 1905 and flatly held minimum wage legislation to be an unconstitutional infringement of the liberty of employers and employees to negotiate employment contracts. Justice Sutherland based his opinion for the Court squarely on *Lochner*. Freedom of contract, he wrote, is "the general rule and restraint the exception."[14] From the standpoint of progressives and reformers, a new dark age had begun.

Ironically, just when the Court emerged in full battle gear to defend the honor of laissez faire capitalism, its services became largely unnec-

---

11. Mason, *The Supreme Court From Taft to Warren*, 50.

12. *See, e.g., Bailey v. Drexel Furniture Co.*, 259 U.S. 20 (1922) (which held the 1919 child labor tax unconstitutional); *Truax v. Corrigan*, 257 U.S. 312 (1921) (which held an Arizona statute restricting labor injunctions unconstitutional); *Duplex Printing Press Co. v. Deering*, 254 U.S. 443 (1921) (which restricted the anti-injunction provisions of the Clayton Act).

13. 261 U.S. 525 (1923).

14. *Id.*, 546. This was too much even for Taft, who dissented. Holmes also dissented. Brandeis did not participate.

essary. The progressive tide receded after 1916, and the nation emerged from World War I in a conservative mood. The hallmarks of the immediate post-war period were anti-subversive witchhunting, racial persecution, America-first isolationism, and economic conservatism. The 1920's were, *par excellence*, the decade of big business. As historian Mason put it:

> To the loud acclaim of the business world, Harding sounded the keynote of the next decade of Republicanism: "We want less government in business and more business in government." The change was highlighted by placing Andrew Mellon, number one businessman, monopolist, and multi-millionaire, at the head of the Treasury Department. The Republican party resigned leadership and practically gave over the government to business. . . . [15]

During this period, businessmen emerged as heroes of popular culture. They dominated government. The prevailing belief was "What's good for business is good for the country." In such a political climate, efforts to regulate business were normally defeated by legislatures, and the services of the Court as guardian of laissez faire were largely unneeded.[16]

Nevertheless, the Taft Court took advantage of opportunity when it arose and nullified twice as many economic regulations as had the Court of the 1910–20 period.[17] Central to this course on which the majority embarked was a conservative attack on the important "property affected with a public interest" doctrine that had been in effect since *Munn v. Illinois*,[18] the landmark 1877 Chicago grain elevator ruling.

In *Munn*, the majority held that government has the power to regulate prices in businesses affected with a public interest. Moreover, *Munn* adopted a liberal, pragmatic approach to the issue, allowing regulation wherever business had some demonstrable impact on the public. The idea that most businesses affect the public and are therefore subject to price regulation remained intact until the 1920's.

Near the end of that decade, however, the Taft Court carried out a conservative counterrevolution in this area of law. The Court ruled that only a very few businesses such as railroads and public utlities are affected with sufficient public interest to warrant regulation. Other enti-

---

15. Mason, *Brandeis, A Free Man's Life*, 530.

16. The prestige of business was immensely strengthened by the economic boom that occurred from 1923 through 1928.

17. McCloskey, *The American Supreme Court*, 158.

18. 97 U.S. 113 (1877). *See supra* p. 69.

ties, including ticket brokers,[19] employment agencies,[20] and the vast majority of all business enterprises, were hence exempt from price regulation. In short, by redefining the term "property affected with a public interest," the Taft Court discarded the traditional general rule permitting price and rate regulation and instituted a new general rule banning such measures.

The Court's liberals, after a period of quiescence, began to challenge these actions. During the first half of the 1920's, they had yielded to Taft's pleas for solidarity and muted their voice of dissent and protest. As the decade waned, however, the good feelings faded. When the country's economic boom started to wind down and hard times approached, the liberal bloc increasingly contested the majority's conservative doctrines. The conservative Justices, and Taft in particular, moved even further to the right. As a result, the Court of the late 1920's polarized into two wings: Taft, McReynolds, Butler, Sutherland, Van Devanter, and Sanford on the right; Holmes, Brandeis, and Stone on the left. Here is Mason's description of the conservative camp's outlook at the time:

> The line drawn between the conservative Right, led by the Chief Justice, and the liberal Left, consisting of Holmes, Brandeis, and Stone, became increasingly sharp. . . .
>
> As his [Taft's] regime neared its end, he grew firm in his belief that the Court must hold the line; it must protect the sacred institutions of property and contract from troublemakers who stimulate popular passion and threaten encroachment. Outsiders, even though they be lawyers, who opposed the "sound," "legal" way or suggested new lines of development—experimentation—were "a lot of sentimentalists," "socialists," "progressives," "bolshevists."
>
> The Chief Justice was alarmed by Dean Roscoe Pound[21] and his sociological jurisprudence. Charles A. Beard, known for his economic interpretation of the Constitution, was brushed off as outstanding among "all the fools I have run across." Brandeis was denounced as "a muckraker, an emotionalist for his own purposes, a Socialist...a man of much power for evil." Even Charles Evans Hughes was suspected of entertaining "a few progressive notions." In contrast, Andrew Mellon was praised as "a long-headed financier," and President Harding extolled for having "on the whole done remarkably well."

---

19. *Tyson v. Banton*, 273 U.S. 416 (1927).
20. *Ribnik v. McBride*, 277 U.S. 350 (1928).
21. Dean of Harvard Law School and leader of the legal realism movement.

Under Taft's leadership, the majority envisioned itself in the van of national progress. The laissez-faire dogma, glorified in the writings of Adam Smith and Herbert Spencer, was the principal avenue to wealth and power. A minimum of lawmaking was raised to the level of an ideal.[22]

The Court's polarization was hardened further by the 1929 stock market collapse and the ensuing collapse of the nation's economy. In the face of a deteriorating economy, the legal and popular sentiments enveloping the Court changed drastically. As in the 1890's, the nation increasingly demanded that government take action to ease the financial crisis. Yet the judicial doctrines developed in the 1920's were for the most part inconsistent with the kind of government action demanded. In short, the Supreme Court was headed for a clash with the nation's legislative and executive institutions.

B. The 1930's and the Hughes Court[23]

After the 1929 stock market collapse, the nation sank into the Great Depression. To the dismay of Chief Justice Taft, even President Herbert Hoover broke with traditional laissez faire policies and attempted, at least on a small scale, to cure the economy by government intervention. But the cure did not take. Inexorably the depression deepened, in 1930, then 1931, then 1932. Demands for massive government action began to bear fruit, first at the state level, then at the federal level as well. But would the Court set aside its conservative, pro-laissez faire views and place the imprimatur of constitutionality on the new economic experiments?

In 1930, two changes in Court personnel created some hope among liberals that the Court would pull back from its rigid conservatism and permit the government to deal with the worsening depression. First, the reactionary Chief Justice Taft died, and Hoover chose Charles Evans Hughes (1910–16, 1930–41) to replace him. Liberals, recalling Hughes' earlier performance as New York's reform governor and Associate Justice of the Supreme Court, and hoping that his subsequent corporate law practice had not destroyed his reforming propensities,

---

22. Mason, *The Supreme Court From Taft to Warren*, 61, 64. Justice Harlan Fiske Stone (1925–46), a giant of Supreme Court history and later Chief Justice, was appointed by President Coolidge to replace McKenna. The best account of Stone's career is A. Mason, *Harlan Fiske Stone: Pillar of the Law* (1956).

23. *See* Galloway, *The Court That Challenged the New Deal (1930–1936)*, 24 Santa Clara L. Rev. 65 (1984).

had some reason to believe Hughes would side with the liberal bloc. Second, the conservative Sanford retired and was replaced by Owen Roberts (1930–45), a former special prosecutor of participants in the Teapot Dome oil scandal. Roberts, a Philadelphia attorney, admittedly looked rather conservative,[24] but the possibility was present that he would provide the fifth vote needed to allow legislatures and executive officers to act.

The two personnel changes of 1930 moved the Court from a solid 6–3 conservative majority to a more ambiguous 4–2–3 split, with four conservatives (Van Devanter, McReynolds, Sutherland, and Butler), three liberals (Holmes, Brandeis, and Stone), and two possible swing votes (Hughes and Roberts). Pfeffer offers this analysis of the 1930 Court:

> Hughes's first entry to the Supreme Court in 1910 inaugurated a period of comparative liberalism, and his re-entry in 1930 appeared to be the harbinger of another revivial of liberalism. On the right, the Praetorian Guard of laissez faire capitalism—McReynolds, Van Devanter, Sutherland, and Butler—were as stalwart and uncompromising as ever. On the left, so too were the avante garde of Brandeis, Stone and Holmes-Cardozo.[25] In the center were Roberts and Hughes, the former perhaps slightly more conservative than Sanford, but the latter far more liberal than Taft. There appeared to be good reason for liberals and progressives to be moderately optimistic as to the future course of the Court.[26]

In the 1932 presidential election, the American people reversed their anti-reformist verdict of 1920. Twelve years of "business as usual" in the private sector and "hands off the economy" on the part of government had resulted in an unprecedented national financial collapse rather than permanent prosperity. Furthermore, when business leaders were asked what to do about combatting the depression, they did not

---

24. In 1923, for example, Roberts gave a speech at a bankers' association meeting attacking the "encroachment of government in American life." 3 Friedman & Israel, *Justices of the United States*, 2255. Although his early voting record showed some moderation, Roberts was a conservative during most of his tenure. His "very last years on the Court reveal a growing conservatism." *Id.*, 2262. At the end he was an "archaic fixture" on the Court. *Id.*, 2263.

25. Holmes retired in 1932. His replacement, Benjamin Nathan Cardozo (1932–38), one of the most respected and beloved Justices in American legal history, was more liberal than Holmes. Thus, the 4–2–3 split was unchanged. No more personnel changes occurred until 1937.

26. Pfeffer, *This Honorable Court*, 291.

know.[27] So the electorate turned to Franklin Delano Roosevelt and his promise of vigorous federal response to the severity of the times.

Immediately after his March 1933 inauguration, Roosevelt redeemed his promise by generating a whirlwind legislative program involving unprecedented federal intervention in the economy. The "100 days" produced even more progressive legislation than the Wilson administration had generated in 1916. In short order, statutes were passed regulating manufacturing (the National Industrial Recovery Act), agriculture (the Agricultural Adjustment Act), the stock market (the Securities Act), banking (the Emergency Banking Act), and other parts of the economy's private sector. Having passed muster in Congress and the White House, Roosevelt's New Deal now faced the stern test of judicial review.

In his book, *The Struggle for Judicial Supremacy*, Robert H. Jackson, the United States Solicitor General who personally briefed and argued the constitutionality of several New Deal measures before the Supreme Court and later became an Associate Justice on the Court, notes, "It was not until 1934 that cases involving governmental power to deal with depression problems caused the Court to speak."[28] Initially, when it did speak, the Court gave some encouragement to the New Dealers. In *Home Bldg. & Loan Ass'n v. Blaisdell*,[29] the Court upheld a Minnesota statute declaring an emergency moratorium on mortgage foreclosures.[30] Hughes wrote the majority opinion. Shortly thereafter, in *Nebbia v. New York*,[31] the Court upheld a New York statute authorizing government regulation of milk prices.[32] Roberts wrote the majority opinion.

Here was hope for Jackson and his fellow New Dealers. Hughes and Roberts, the two new swing votes, had sided with the liberals, Brandeis, Stone, and Cardozo, in sustaining government power to deal with the hard times. On the other hand, the Court's conservative Justices, who eventually acquired the moniker "the four horsemen," dissented as a bloc in both cases. Said Jackson:

---

27. Schlesinger, *The Crisis of the Old Order*, 457.

28. Jackson, *The Struggle for Judicial Supremacy*, 78.

29. 290 U.S. 398 (1934).

30. Protection against foreclosure on debts during hard times had, of course, been a consistent reform proposal since the days of Shays' Rebellion.

31. 291 U.S. 502 (1934).

32. *Nebbia* reinstated the broad definition of "businesses affected with a public interest" established by *Munn v. Illinois, see supra* p. 69, and cancelled the Taft Court's restrictive definition, *see supra* pp. 107–08.

Four of the Justices, Van Devanter, Sutherland, McReynolds, and Butler, within one of a majority, were asserting a power and duty in the judiciary to stop any governing body—state or federal—from interfering
with an economy of laissez faire.[33]

Obviously, if either Hughes or Roberts joined forces with the conservatives, the New Deal was in trouble.

In 1935, the tenuous liberal-moderate coalition disintegrated, and
the Supreme Court began to void the New Deal by declaring many of
its key statutory underpinnings unconstitutional.[34] Justice Roberts
moved sharply to the right into close alignment with the four horsemen. Chief Justice Hughes additionally joined the conservatives in
about half the subsequent closely divided rulings. In a few instances,
even the liberals banded together with their conservative counterparts
in nullifying New Deal legislation. But by far the worst damage to Roosevelt's economic recovery programs was done by Roberts and the four
horsemen, often over bloc dissents by the Court's liberal wing.

The string of cases involving constitutional challenges to New Deal
statutes in the 1935–36 period is long and fascinating. At the outset
came *Panama Refining Co. v. Ryan*,[35] overturning a federal statute designed to regulate the oil industry. The liberals won *Norman v. Baltimore & O. Ry. Co.*,[36] which, by a 5–4 vote, upheld the Emergency
Banking Act provision voiding so-called "gold clauses" in contracts
and allowing payment of debts in legal tender. The conservative trend
picked up again with *Railroad Retirement Bd. v. Alton R.R. Co.*,[37] in
which Roberts joined the four horsemen in condemning the Railroad
Retirement Act of 1934, which provided for railroad worker pen-
sions.[38]

The full-scale disaster for Roosevelt's economic relief and recovery
programs hit on the last day of the October 1934 Term, May 27, 1935.
On that day, which Jackson named "Black Monday," the Bench declared three especially important New Deal initiatives unconstitutional. In *Louisville Bank v. Radford*,[39] the Court nullified the Frazier-
Lemke Act, which provided much needed relief for farm mortgagors.

---

33. Jackson, *The Struggle for Judicial Supremacy*, 82.
34. *Id.*, 86–123.
35. 293 U.S. 389 (1935).
36. 294 U.S. 240 (1935).
37. 295 U.S. 330 (1935).
38. Hughes, Brandeis, Stone, and Cardozo dissented.
39. 295 U.S. 555 (1935).

In *Humphrey's Executor v. United States*,[40] the majority held that Roosevelt was without power to remove a reactionary Federal Trade Commission member from official service. And, in the most famous decision of the three, *Schechter Poultry Corp. v. United States*,[41] the Court threw out the National Industrial Recovery Act , the heart of the New Deal's initial effort to deal with industrial unemployment and lack of production. Further, following the Supreme Court's lead, lower courts began enjoining economic reform efforts by Congress and executive officers. In 1935 and 1936 alone, "sixteen hundred injunctions restraining officers of the Federal Government from carrying out acts of Congress were granted by Federal Judges."[42]

The attack on the New Deal continued throughout the October 1935 Term as well.[43] On January 6, 1936, the Court handed down *United States v. Butler*[44] holding the Agricultural Adjustment Act unconstitutional. Jackson described this decision, in which both Hughes and Roberts sided with the four horsemen, as a "crushing disappointment to the Administration."[45] The A.A.A., which provided desperately needed price supports and subsidies for farmers, had been one of the major causes of the rural recovery that took root in America from 1933 to 1935. Yet, the attorney for the A.A.A.'s opponents, George Wharton Pepper, speaking in tones reminiscent of Choate in the 1895 income tax case, charged that approval of the measure would be equivalent to the end of freedom:

> Indeed, may it please your Honors, I believe I am standing here today to plead the cause of the America I have loved; and I pray Almighty God that not in my time may "the land of the regimented" be accepted as a worthy substitute for "the land of the free."[46]

The Court's opinion declaring the A.A.A. unconstitutional was based on the concept that the nation's agriculture was a local problem over which the federal government had no power whatever. In so holding, the Court temporarily rendered the Roosevelt administration impotent to deal with the crucial problem of food production.

---

40. 295 U.S. 602 (1935).
41. 295 U.S. 495 (1935).
42. Jackson, *The Struggle for Judicial Supremacy*, 115.
43. *Id.*, 124–75.
44. 297 U.S. 1 (1936).
45. Jackson, *The Struggle for Judicial Supremacy*, 125.
46. 297 U.S. at 44.

The next disaster for the New Deal was *Jones v. SEC.*[47] The issue was whether an individual charged with stock fraud under the Securities Act could escape investigation, exposure, and punishment simply by withdrawing the registration statement containing the false representations. In a 6–3 decision, the Court struck an almost disabling blow at the SEC by holding that withdrawal of the statement prevented the SEC from taking any further action. Moreover, Justice Sutherland's majority opinion strongly condemned the SEC's behavior.

The *Jones* case was followed by *Carter v. Carter Coal Co.,*[48] which held the Bituminous Coal Conservation Act unconstitutional. The statute was particularly important for the New Deal, since it dealt with problems in the coal mining industry that had in turn led to severe disorders and extreme misery on the part of the miners. Writing for the majority, Justice Sutherland declared the statute unconstitutional as an improper delegation of law-making power from Congress to the White House.

After then declaring the Municipal Bankruptcy Law unconstitutional,[49] the Court finished off its term by striking down New York's Minimum Wage Law for Women in *Morehead v. New York* ex rel. *Tipaldo.*[50] Using, in by now almost classic style, the "substantive due process/freedom of contract" concept as a buttress against wage and hour legislation, Justice Butler, speaking for the five-vote majority, followed this conservative line:

> In making contracts of employment, generally speaking, the parties have equal right to obtain from each other the best terms they can by private bargaining. Legislative abridgement of that freedom can only be justified by the existence of exceptional circumstances. Freedom of contract is the general rule and restraint the exception.[51]

As Jackson stated in his account of the case:

> This, of course, meant that the weak must bear the consequences of their weakness, and the strong may drive the best bargain that their strength and labor's necessities make possible. Labor relations were to be governed by the law of the jungle, and the state might not protect even women and children from exploitation.[52]

---

47. 298 U.S. 1 (1936).
48. 298 U.S. 238 (1936).
49. *Ashton v. Cameron County Dist.,* 298 U.S. 513 (1936).
50. 298 U.S. 587 (1936).
51. *Id.,* 610–11.
52. Jackson, *The Struggle for Judicial Supremacy,* 172.

In his dissenting opinion, Justice Stone made much the same point. He wrote:

> There is grim irony in speaking of the freedom of contract of those who, because of their economic necessities, give their services for less than is needful to keep body and soul together. But if this is freedom of contract no one has ever denied that it is freedom which may be restrained, notwithstanding the Fourteenth Amendment, by a statute passed in the public interest.[53]

In short, during the mid-1930's, the Court carried out a systematic attack on the New Deal, nullifying many of the leading legislative and executive efforts at economic reform. With the four horsemen leading the way and Roberts close behind, the forces of laissez faire conservatism swept to victory in case after case. Most of the cases were decided by narrow 5–4 or 6–3 margins, but even the liberals deserted Roosevelt's standard by repudiating the National Industrial Recovery Act and signalling the executive and legislative branches that the collectivist program of the so-called First New Deal was unacceptable to the Court. A constitutional impasse was at hand.

Table 16 shows how the Justices tended to split during this period when the decisions were not unanimous.

TABLE 16
Alignment of Justices, 1935–36

Left	Center	Right
Brandeis	Hughes	McReynolds
Cardozo		Butler
Stone		Van Devanter
		Sutherland
		Roberts

In its attack on the New Deal, the Supreme Court majority relied most often on four conceptual weapons: 1) economic substantive due process, the doctrine that unreasonable statutes violate due process, 2) dual federalism, the doctrine that the tenth amendment bars federal regulation of local activities such as manufacturing, 3) restrictive interpretations of the scope of federal powers, especially the commerce power, and 4) the notion that Congress may not delegate broad rule-

---

53. 298 U.S. at 632.

making authority to executive agencies. Substantive due process was used to destroy the Frazier-Lemke Act (farm mortgage relief) in *Radford* and the New York Minimum Wage Law for Women in *Tipaldo*. Dual federalism and the restrictive interpretation of the commerce power were the bases for the overthrow of the A.A.A., the Bituminous Coal Conservation Act, the Municipal Bankruptcy Act, and the National Industrial Recovery Act in the *Butler, Carter, Ashton,* and *Schechter* cases. Unlawful delegation of legislative power provided a basis for the nullification of the N.I.R.A. and the "hot oil" statute in the *Schechter* and *Ryan* cases.

As Jackson summarized the situation:

> Two kinds of power seem always in competition in our democracy: there is political power, which is the power of the voters, and there is the economic power of property, which is the power of its owners. Conflicts between the two bring much grist to the judicial mill. The basic grievance of the New Deal was that the Court seemed alway unduly to favor private economic power and to find ways of circumventing the efforts of popular government to control or regulate it.
>
> Thus, as we shall see, the Court conducted a dual campaign against the powers which the Congress thought had been granted to it by the Constitution. On the one hand, it *narrowed* the scope of the great clauses of the Constitution granting powers to Congress. It seriously contracted the interstate commerce power and it read startling exemptions into the taxing power. Simultaneously, it *expanded* the scope of clauses which limited the power of Congress, such as the "due process clause" and the clauses withholding power from the federation. At the same time it used the "due process" concept to cut down the effective power of the states. Divisions of opinion on constitutional interpretation ceased to be along the classic lines of a liberal as against a strict construction. The same justices used both in the interests of private economic power: they were strict and niggardly in construing the powers of government and liberal to the point of extravagance in construing such limitations as "freedom of contract" where none existed in the Constitution.
>
> It was this manifestation of judicial supremacy which threatened legislative and executive paralysis and provoked the revolt against the Court's prevailing doctrine.[54]

---

54. Jackson, *The Struggle for Judicial Supremacy,* xii–xiii.

Part Five
The Second Liberal Era (1937–1969)

11

The Constitutional Revolution of 1937[1]

It was not recognized at the time, but the Tipaldo case marked the end of the Court that Marshall had created. When the Justices left for their summer vacation in June of 1936 they almost certainly did not anticipate that never again (at least until 1965, the time of the present writing) would the Court employ the Constitution to interfere in any substantial extent with government of economic affairs. The era of judicial nullification of social welfare laws had come to an end.[2]

The year 1937 marks, by all odds, the single most decisive turning point in the history of American constitutional law. The judicial events of that year fully merit the label "revolutionary," since they involved renunciation by the Court of the very activity that had been its most important and characteristic function for nearly 50 years, namely the exercise of a constitutional veto over economic legislation.

The stage for the constitutional revolution of 1937 was set by the national election of 1936. The people of the nation then, by a popular margin of nearly 8,000,000 votes and an electoral college margin of 523 to 8, ratified the New Deal and returned Franklin Delano Roosevelt to office with a mandate for massive government intervention designed to end the hard times and get the nation on its economic feet again. Yet, as Roosevelt returned to his task, he faced a Court that had persistently denied the nation's authority to undertake the economic experiment the people wanted. A constitutional impasse had developed.

On February 5, 1937, Roosevelt launched an attack on the Court by proposing legislation to increase the number of Justices from nine to fifteen and thus provide enough additional pro-New Deal votes to overthrow the dominance of the old guard on the Court.[3] In other words,

---

1. *See* Jackson, *The Struggle for Judicial Supremacy*, 176–285.

2. Pfeffer, *This Honorable Court*, 310.

3. In his initial message to Congress, Roosevelt tried to skirt the real issue by claiming that the reason for adding new Justices was merely to provide more energy for the burdened Court. On March 9, 1937, however, Roosevelt admitted to the nation that the real purpose was to change the law.

Roosevelt threatened to "pack" the Court. All eyes turned to the Bench to see what the reaction would be.

Court watchers did not have long to wait. On March 29, 1937, in one of the most astounding turnabouts in American legal history, the Court upheld the State of Washington's minimum wage act for women, a statute "which was substantially identical to the New York Act declared unconstitutional [in *Tipaldo*] only the year before."[4] The decision, which as much as any other mentioned in this text merits the title of landmark case, was *West Coast Hotel Co. v. Parrish*.[5]

Elsie Parrish was a "chambermaid" at the West Coast Hotel. The hotel paid Ms. Parrish wages that did not satisfy Washington's statute. She sued for the difference. The hotel argued that the statute violated substantive due process, citing *Adkins v. Children's Hospital*[6] and *Tipaldo*.[7] No doubt, under prior case law, the hotel was correct. *Adkins*, which had used substantive due process to invalidate the District of Columbia minimum wage law, also involved a woman employed in a hotel. Moreover, *Tipaldo* had reaffirmed *Adkins* only the prior term. Predictably, a lower court had already dismissed the case once.

The Supreme Court, by a narrow 5–4 margin, shocked the legal community by upholding the Washington minimum wage law. "[I]f such laws," the majority stated, "have a reasonable relation to a proper legislative purpose, and are neither arbitrary nor discriminatory, the requirements of due process are satisfied. . . . "[8] The principle was not new. It was the familiar rational relation test that the pre-1937 Court had used with such vengeance. The revolutionary dimension inherent in the ruling was the Court's explicit adoption of a deferential attitude in applying the test. A strong presumption of constitutionality, the Court held, applies to statutes regulating employment contracts, even when they restrict the liberty of employers and employees to set wages and hours of employment. As the majority put it:

> In dealing with the relation of employer and employed, the legislature had necessarily a wide field of discretion. . . . [A statute regulating such a relationship] may not be annulled unless palpably in excess of legislative power. . . . [E]very possible presumption is in favor of its validity. . . .[9]

---

4. Jackson, *The Struggle for Judicial Supremacy*, 191.
5. 300 U.S. 379 (1937).
6. 261 U.S. 525 (1923). *See supra* p. 106.
7. 298 U.S. 587 (1936). *See supra* pp. 114–15.
8. 300 U.S. at 398.
9. *Id.*, 398, 400.

This, of course, was directly contrary to *Adkins*, which held, "Freedom of contract is . . . the general rule and restraint the exception."[10] And that was precisely the revolutionary change. Applying their new deferential rational basis test, five Justices found Washington's minimum wage law reasonable. The majority ended its opinion by explicitly overruling *Adkins*. The four horsemen, to no one's surprise, dissented.

West Coast Hotel Co. v. Parrish merits attention not only because it was the first major decision in the constitutional revolution of 1937 but even more because the ruling destroyed the centerpiece of conservative constitutional activism, economic substantive due process. This doctrine had been the pre-1937 Court's most powerful weapon in the battle against state economic reform legislation. By converting the old presumption of unconstitutionality of economic statutes into a strong, opposite presumption of constitutionality, *Parrish* brought to a close the era of conservative due process activism that had persisted since 1890.

Any feeling that *Parrish* might be only a momentary respite for the New Deal was laid to rest by subsequent cases. A mere two weeks later, on April 12, 1937, the Court announced the important decision in *National Labor Relations Board v. Jones & Laughlin Steel Corp.*,[11] which dramatically expanded federal power to regulate commerce, upheld the National Labor Relations Act, and provided "the most far-reaching victory ever won on behalf of labor in the Supreme Court."[12] The Court then proceeded before the end of the term to sustain both state and federal unemployment compensation laws and the old-age benefit provisions of the federal Social Security Act.[13] The usual split in these cases was 5–4, with Brandeis, Stone, Cardozo, Hughes, and Roberts *versus* Van Devanter, McReynolds, Sutherland, and Butler.

The basic constitutional policy that captured the Court in 1937 has remained dominant to the present day. According to this doctrine, it is not proper for the judiciary to nullify duly enacted state or federal economic statutes simply because the Justices believe they unreasonably interfere with economic liberty or with matters of allegedly local concern. Henceforth, property rights were demoted from the preferred, al-

---

10. 261 U.S. 525, 546 (1923).
11. 301 U.S. 1 (1937).
12. Jackson, *The Struggle for Judicial Supremacy*, 214.
13. *Carmichael v. Southern Coal Co.*, 301 U.S. 495 (1937) (state unemployment insurance); *Steward Machine Co. v. Davis*, 301 U.S. 548 (1937) (federal unemployment compensation); *Helvering v. Davis*, 301 U.S. 619 (1937) (old-age benefits).

most sacred, position they had held since the days of philosopher John Locke and placed alongside the other interests which are subject to adjustment and compromise through the legislative process.

How could this fundamental change occur without a single change in Court personnel? The answer is surprisingly simple, albeit somewhat disillusioning for those who believe the law should be based on stable principles of reason: one Justice changed his mind.

Immediately prior to 1937, three Supreme Court Justices had led the opposition to the dominant theme of laissez faire, Brandeis, Stone, and Cardozo. During the 1935 Term, the unpredictable Chief Justice Hughes had vacillated between the Court's liberal and conservative wings, often leaving only the narrowest 5–4 margin favoring the conservative view. All that was needed to create the revolution was for one Justice to change sides. That one Justice turned out to be Owen Roberts, who affiliated with the liberals in *West Coast Hotel v. Parrish*[14] and subsequent cases, giving them the majority they had so long lacked.

Shortly thereafter, events occurred insuring that the constitutional revolution of 1937 would be a durable one. Perhaps sensing their cause was doomed, the old guard began to retire. The first to go was Justice Van Devanter, who departed at the end of the October 1936 Term. Van Devanter had served as a reliable member of the four horsemen, and his loss left a gaping hole in their ranks. Roosevelt then stunned conservatives by appointing "people's lawyer" Hugo Lafayette Black (1937–71), a man who was far to the left of even Justice Brandeis.[15] During 1938, Justice Sutherland followed Van Devanter into retirement and

---

14. Roberts' shift from the conservative majority in *Tipaldo* to the liberal majority in *Parrish* was dubbed the "switch in time that saved nine."

15. For a particularly intimate account of Justice Black's life and thought, see H. Black, Jr., *My Father* (1975). In his book, Hugo Black, Jr., describes his father as an economic radical who believed the government should support the common people in their endless struggle to combat the exploitative systems created by concentrated wealth. *Id.*, 140 *et seq.* Justice Black believed, "[T]he combined power of organized wealth and its organized propaganda never ceases to fight every intelligent effort to save us from terrible abuses incident to the exploitation of the many by the powerful few." *Id.*, 147.

Black distrusted wealth, distrusted businessmen, opposed depreciation deductions and the inheritance of wealth, and rejected the traditional conservative trickle down theory. "We don't have to bribe the rich to let them get richer." *Id.*, 146. "Daddy . . . determined to do all he could to make the Supreme Court a haven for the helpless, weak. . . ." *Id.*, 182. Black was the most liberal member of the Court when he was seated, and he remained a member of the Court's liberal wing until the last few years of his long tenure.

was replaced by another New Dealer, Stanley F. Reed (1938–57).[16] These and later Roosevelt appointments eradicated all possibilities of an immediate counterrevolution.

The fabric of the new majority's economic jurisprudence was woven out of several key doctrinal strands. The doctrine of economic substantive due process and the related doctrine of liberty of contract were almost completely discarded.[17] The commerce clause was invested once more with the broad sweep that Chief Justice Marshall had established more than a century earlier.[18] Other federal powers were given a similarly broad interpretation, including the taxing and spending powers, the war power, and the foreign relations powers.[19] The notion that the tenth amendment restricts the federal government by reserving large areas of legislative action exclusively for the States was rejected.[20] The doctrine of unconstitutional delegation of legislative power was substantially loosened.[21]

The Court's deferential attitude toward economic legislation applied not only to the federal government but to the States as well. The reduction of substantive due process/liberty of contract restrictions freed the States from far-reaching restraints[22] as did the softening of dormant commerce clause restrictions.[23] In short, the Roosevelt Court withdrew from the role of constitutional censor of socio-economic legislation, adopting instead the posture of judicial restraint characteristic of Holmesian liberalism.

The turnabout marked a milestone and major victory for the poor in their struggle for greater opportunity at the bar of the Supreme Court.

---

16. Reed was far more liberal than Sutherland, whom he replaced, but he was "no left winger." Pfeffer, *This Honorable Court*, 330.

17. *E.g.*, *State Tax Comm'n v. Aldrich*, 316 U.S. 174 (1942); *Olsen v. Nebraska*, 313 U.S. 236 (1941); *Curry v. McCanless*, 307 U.S. 104 (1939); *West Coast Hotel v. Parrish*, 300 U.S. 379 (1937).

18. *E.g.*, *American Power & Light Co. v. SEC*, 329 U.S. 90 (1946); *Wickard v. Filburn*, 317 U.S. 111 (1942); *Mulford v. Smith*, 307 U.S. 38 (1939); *NLRB v. Jones & Laughlin Steel Corp.*, 301 U.S. 1 (1937).

19. *E.g.*, *Helvering v. Davis*, 301 U.S. 619 (1937) (taxing and spending powers); *Steward Machine Co. v. Davis*, 301 U.S. 548 (1937) (taxing and spending powers).

20. *E.g.*, *United States v. Darby Lumber Co.*, 312 U.S. 100 (1941).

21. *E.g.*, *Yakus v. United States*, 321 U.S. 414 (1944); *H. P. Hood & Sons v. United States*, 307 U.S. 588 (1939).

22. *See* cases cited *supra* note 17, this chapter.

23. *E.g.*, *Nelson v. Sears, Roebuck & Co.*, 312 U.S. 359 (1941); *McGoldrick v. Berwind-White Coal Co.*, 309 U.S. 33 (1940); *South Carolina Highway Dept. v. Barnwell Bros.*, 303 U.S. 177 (1938).

No longer would the advocates of economic reform need to fear that their hard-won legislative victories would be nullified by conservative Supreme Court Justices.

Although this constitutional revolution, for all practical purposes, eliminated the old economic issues from consideration, it did not eliminate rich-poor issues from the Supreme Court's docket. However, the specific issues changed. Henceforth, the Court's greatest impact in the economic arena derived from its authority to interpret and enforce legislation. Since it is often impossible to draft completely unambiguous statutes, the Supreme Court retains substantial power to control the impact of socio-economic legislation through the alchemy of judicial interpretation. Moreover, important new issues having indirect but significant impacts on the rich-poor struggle emerged in the post-1937 period, issues concerning race relations, voting rights, criminal procedure, and the like. These issues were destined to provide opportunities for new and less conspicuous forms of economic liberalism and conservatism to appear.

12

The Roosevelt Court
(1937–1946)[1]

Roosevelt's initial triumph in acquiring for his New Deal programs the judicial approval he had sought for so long was achieved without his having to make a single change in Court personnel. He was soon able, however, to reinforce his accomplishment by engineering what was perhaps the most dramatic political and philosophical shift among the nine Justices ever to occur in a relatively short period of American history.

Between 1937 and 1943, Roosevelt made eight appointments to the Court,[2] beginning with Hugo Black, the most liberal person to serve as Justice up to that time, and Stanley Reed, the Solicitor General who had represented the government in many Court challenges to New Deal programs.

In the years after the two were seated, openings on the Court continued to come thick and fast. In 1938, Cardozo died. He was succeeded by Felix Frankfurter (1939–62), a political liberal, important Roosevelt advisor, and draftsman of much New Deal legislation.[3] That same year, Brandeis retired. Roosevelt named to his seat the equally liberal William O. Douglas (1939–75), another New Deal brain truster, who had served previously on the SEC.[4] In 1939, a third member of the con-

---

1. *See* Galloway, *The Roosevelt Court: The Liberals Conquer (1937–1941) and Divide (1941–1946)*, 23 Santa Clara L. Rev. 491 (1983). The best book on this period of Supreme Court history is C. Prichett, *The Roosevelt Court* (1948).

2. Other than Roosevelt, only George Washington made this many appointments.

3. Among the extensive literature on Frankfurter, the following are of special interest: B. Murphy, *The Brandeis/Frankfurter Connection* (1982); M. Parrish, *Felix Frankfurter and His Times: The Reform Years* (1982); H. Phillips, *Felix Frankfurter Reminisces* (1960). Frankfurter was one of the most politically liberal men appointed by Roosevelt. However, because of a deeply rooted Holmesian belief in judicial restraint, Frankfurter became a conservative Justice. Thus, the Cardozo-Frankfurter succession was a minor shift to the right, the only one among the Roosevelt personnel changes.

4. Douglas was a "champion of the weak against the strong." Black, *My Father*, 242. As Justice Black put it, "He'll always vote for a labor union, because he thinks

servative old guard, Justice Butler, died. To fill the vacancy, Roosevelt selected still another reformer, Michigan's liberal ex-governor Frank Murphy.[5] Roosevelt's appointees were now a majority on the Court.

In 1941, moderate Chief Justice Charles Evans Hughes retired. His position was filled by the promotion of Harlan F. Stone, who had been affiliated with the Court's liberal wing ever since his appointment in 1925. The seat vacated by the promotion went to Roosevelt's Attorney General and former Solicitor General, Robert H. Jackson (1941–54).[6] Finally, the last of the four horsemen, McReynolds, retired. James F. Byrnes (1941–42), one of Roosevelt's closest political confidantes, was appointed to replace him. Byrnes chose to serve on the Court for only one year, after which he was succeed by Wiley Rutledge (1943–49), another strong liberal.[7] For the next six years, the "libertarian four," Black, Douglas, Murphy, and Rutledge, comprised a powerful liberal-activist bloc.

Table 17 illustrates the remarkable shift in judicial viewpoints on purely economic matters brought about by Roosevelt.

---

government has got to sponsor power to countervail against privilege." *Id.* A first-hand account of Douglas' deep identification with the poor can be found in his autobiography, where he stated he was "aligned . . . emotionally with the miserable people who make up the chaff of society." W. Douglas, *Go East, Young Man,* (1974), 62. Douglas grew up in abject poverty, and this theme of identification with the poor comes through many times in his writings. To cite only one more example: "My heart was with the impoverished, restless underdogs who were the IWW's." *Id.,* 78. Douglas was the Court's most liberal Justice for more than twenty years at the end of his tenure.

5. *See* 4 Friedman & Israel, *The Justices of the United States,* 2493–2506. Murphy soon became a member of the liberal-activist wing along with Black and Douglas. In fact, he was arguably "the most militant liberal on the Court." *Id.,* 2668. "He had been an ardent New Dealer and on the bench he aligned himself with Black and Douglas as a steadfast champion of civil liberties." Pfeffer, *This Honorable Court,* 342.

6. Once on the Court, Jackson joined the Frankfurter-Reed wing. The following quotes concerning labor and judicial restraint illustrate Jackson's moderate, restrained position. "[M]y feeling [was] that labor was no more to be trusted than capital to conform its policies to good social practices. . . ." 4 Friedman & Israel, *The Justices of the United States,* 2551. "In general I agreed with Chief Justice Stone that activism was no more appropriate on the part of the judiciary in favor of reforms than it was in knocking them down." *Id.,* 2565.

7. Rutledge was an "outspoken defender of the 'underdog.'" 4 Friedman & Israel, *The Justices of the United States,* 2595. He was an economic liberal, favorable toward the New Deal, favorable toward powerful regulatory agencies, favorable toward labor. "On the bench Rutledge aligned himself with Black, Douglas and Murphy as a staunch champion . . . of the 1937 revolution." Pfeffer, *This Honorable Court,* 346.

TABLE 17
Alignment of Justices, 1943

Left	Center	Right
Murphy	Roberts[8]	
Rutledge		
Black		
Douglas		
Reed		
Frank-		
furter		
Jackson		
Stone		

Clearly, the Court's second conservative era was finished. By 1943 the assembly serving on the Court was the most liberal in the Court's history.[9] The Bench's second liberal era was well underway.

The first task awaiting the Roosevelt majority was simply to confirm the rule of judicial restraint in economic cases established in 1937. This job was carried out in a consistent and explicit manner, leaving no doubt that the Court had withdrawn from its prior role as constitutional censor of economic legislation.

In 1939, for example, the Court upheld the Agricultural Adjustment Act of 1938, which, among other things, set production quotas for tobacco producers.[10] Such regulations of local production would not have survived the Court's scrutiny during the early 1930's. In 1939, the Court sustained the power of Congress to delegate to the Department of Agriculture broad authority to regulate prices of goods moving in interstate commerce.[11] Similarly, "the Court sustained the constitutionality of a municipal bankruptcy law in all essentials the same as one it had held unconstitutional two years before."[12] These and other similar cases attest to the validity of Pfeffer's assertion that after 1937, "the

8. Roberts is listed as a moderate here because of his change of position in early 1937. He was previously listed as a conservative. *See supra* p. 115.

9. The Taney Court after 1837 may have been as liberal on occasion. No other Court is even in contention.

10. *Mulford v. Smith*, 307 U.S. 38 (1939).

11. *United States v. Rock Royal Co-op*, 307 U.S. 533 (1939).

12. *United States v. Bekins*, 304 U.S. 27 (1938). The quote is from Jackson, *The Struggle for Judicial Supremacy*, 240.

era of judicial nullification of social welfare laws had come to an end."[13]

A case which epitomizes the constitutional posture of the Roosevelt Court in the economic arena is *United States v. F. W. Darby Lumber Co.*,[14] the landmark case that upheld the federal Fair Labor Standards Act of 1938. The statute was the last major New Deal economic reform statute. It imposed sweeping wage and hour restraints on businesses affecting interstate commerce. Prior to 1937, this statute would have been held to violate substantive due process and the tenth amendment and to exceed Congress' power under the commerce clause. Stone's majority opinion in *Darby* rejected each of these theories in forceful terms.

Substantive due process was brushed aside in the following curt passage: "Since our decision in *West Coast Hotel v. Parrish* ... it is no longer open to question that the fixing of a minimum wage is within the legislative power. ... Nor is it any longer open to question that it is within the legislative power to fix maximum hours."[15] The pre-1937 notion of dual federalism derived from the tenth amendment was rejected in even stronger terms: "Our conclusion is unaffected by the Tenth Amendment. ... The amendment states but a truism. ... [F]or many years the amendment has been construed as not depriving the national government of authority to resort to all means for the exercise of a granted power which are appropriate and plainly adapted to the permitted end."[16] Finally, the Court adopted an extremely broad reading of the "plenary power conferred on Congress by the Commerce Clause."[17] Holding that Congress has broad power to regulate even local activities which affect interstate commerce, the Court stated, "The power of Congress over interstate commerce is complete in itself, may be exercised to its utmost extent, and acknowledges no limitations other than are prescribed in the Constitution."[18]

The *Darby* opinion was, then, a veritable graveyard for the leading economic ideas of the pre-1937 Court. Moreover, the ruling indicated

---

13. Pfeffer, *This Honorable Court*, 310.

14. 312 U.S. 100 (1941).

15. *Id.*, 125.

16. *Id.*, 123–24.

17. *Id.*, 115.

18. *Id.*, 114. Cf. *Wickard v. Filburn*, 317 U.S. 311 (1942), holding that Congress may regulate local activities which, in the aggregate, arguably affect interstate commerce.

that fair labor standards, including minimum wage and maximum hour regulations, had reached a milestone in their long and circuitous journey through the courts and had apparently arrived at a safe constitutional haven.

The Roosevelt Court's enthusiasm for the administration's brand of economic thinking went far beyond merely discarding pre-1937 constitutional restraints on socio-economic legislation. There still remained the vastly important task of construing and enforcing the sweeping legislation characteristic of the age of big government. Here the majority took the position that these measures were to be broadly construed. Again and again, the prevailing Justices insisted upon vigorous enforcement of economic reform statutes, giving especially strong support to legislative and executive programs of business and trade regulation.[19]

The Court's economic liberalism was perhaps most evident in cases involving labor unions.[20] Roughly a decade and a half earlier, Chief Justice Taft had described labor unions as a group the Court had to "hit every little while" to keep them in line. The Roosevelt Court, in contrast, took such an opposite tack as to lead the greatest constitutional scholar of the period, Edward S. Corwin, to write in 1946, "Constitutional law has always had a central interest to guard. Today it appears to be that of organized labor."[21]

Among the pro-labor cases leading to Corwin's conclusion were *Apex Hosiery v. Leader*,[22] which overturned a long string of precedents and held union activities to be exempt from the "restraint of trade" prohibitions of the Sherman Act, and *Thornhill v. Alabama*,[23] which held peaceful picketing to be a protected form of speech under the first

---

19. *E.g., Gemsco, Inc. v. Walling*, 324 U.S. 244 (1945) (Administrator, FLSA); *FPC v. Hope Natural Gas Co.*, 320 U.S. 591 (1944) (FPC); *NBC v. United States*, 319 U.S. 190 (1943) (FCC); *FPC v. Natural Gas Pipeline Co.*, 315 U.S. 575 (1942) (FPC); *Gray v. Powell*, 314 U.S. 402 (1941) (Bituminous Coal Division); *United States v. Morgan*, 313 U.S. 409 (1941) (USDA). *See* Pritchett, *The Roosevelt Court*, 167–97, which discusses "[t]he generally favorable attitude of the Roosevelt Court toward administrative legislation." *Id.*, 168.

20. Another major area was civil rights and civil liberties. After 1937, the attention of the judicial "activists" turned increasingly toward protecting interests of minorities and of individuals harmed by the government.

21. E. Corwin, *The Constitution and What it Means Today* (1965), vii.

22. 310 U.S. 469 (1940).

23. 310 U.S. 88 (1940).

amendment. The days when the wealthy could look to the Supreme Court as the final bastion against the efforts of the masses to redistribute power and property were gone—at least for the time being.[24]

But, for all the radical changes they wrought in judicial thinking as regards the roles and responsibilities of government's various branches, it would be mistaken to conclude that the New Deal Justices were continually of one mind on all issues. True, the most moderate of Roosevelt's appointees were far more liberal than the four horsemen who preceded them and, true, the President's first five appointees, Black, Reed, Frankfurter, Douglas, and Murphy, tended to vote overwhelmingly as a bloc during the 1937–39 period.[25] Nevertheless, after 1940, the Justices began slowly to split into two distinct groups, one reflecting a spirit of judicial activism, the other tempered by a belief in judicial restraint. Black and Douglas were charter members of the activist faction. Murphy soon joined them, and Rutledge came aboard in 1943. Frankfurter and Reed were the earliest Roosevelt appointee's to join Stone's "moderation through restraint" opposition. They were soon joined by Jackson. Meanwhile, Roberts drifted in the direction of increased conservatism. As a result, the Court line-up from 1943 to 1945 was as follows:

TABLE 18
Alignment of Justices, 1943–45

Left	Center	Right
Murphy	Reed	Roberts
Rutledge	Jackson	
Douglas	Frankfurter	
Black	Stone	

So, as World War II was drawing to a close, and as Roosevelt's death approached, the question of how far the Justices should go in pursuing liberal goals was becoming the central economic issue for the Court.

---

24. The Roosevelt Court was also relatively liberal in civil liberties cases. During World War II, the Court's vigilance helped keep the nation from falling into the kind of reactionary period that occurred toward the end of World War I. However, the Court's defense of civil liberties faltered a few years later, when the Cold War began and McCarthyism emerged.

25. Black and Douglas, for example, agreed in 335 cases before recording their first disagreement. Black and Frankfurter, later known as leaders of the Court's opposite wings, agreed in 199 of their first 202 cases. Reed agreed with the others in roughly 95% of the cases during this period. *See* Galloway, *The Supreme Court Since 1937*, 24 Santa Clara L. Rev. 565, 570 (1984).

13

The Vinson Court (1946–1953)[1]

During the late 1940's, the United States entered a period of political and economic conservatism. After World War II, instead of peace came "Cold War." The communist nations, which had been allied with America in the struggle against Nazi Germany, now appeared to many as a monolithic force bent on subjugating the entire world. The United States underwent a kind of collective psychosis in which subversives were suspected of hiding behind every bush and under every table. The hysteria took hold in the late 1940's and climaxed in the early 1950's, when Senator Joseph McCarthy dominated the nation as few individuals have ever done and held power to destroy the reputations and often the economic well-being of persons he accused of being communists or communist sympathizers.

The prevailing conservative mood spilled over into the political arena in a variety of ways. In the 1946 off-year elections, the Republicans took control of both houses of Congress and soon enacted legislation "that expressed the general conservative reaction against the New Deal era."[2] Anti-labor sentiment produced the Taft-Hartley Act of 1947, which banned the closed shop and imposed liability on unions for breaches of collective bargaining agreements. Truman's "Fair Deal" economic reform package, an aggregate of agricultural, labor, and civil rights measures, died in Congress. As the years passed, advocacy of economic reform carried with it the risk of being blacklisted, which in turn often meant a loss of employment and community status.

The reactionary drift of the McCarthy Era was so powerful that no Court could have deflected it from its course. Nevertheless, an activist set of Justices might have curbed at least some of its excesses. The Court of the McCarthy Era, however, was of a significantly different stripe from its immediate predecessor. Eventually bolstered by four surprisingly conservative Truman appointees, the Court's more con-

---

1. For more detailed discussions of the Vinson era, see C. Pritchett, *Civil Liberties and the Vinson Court* (1954); Galloway, *The Vinson Court: Polarization (1946–1949) and Conservative Dominance (1949–1953)*, 22 Santa Clara L. Rev. 375 (1982).

2. 2 R. Hofstadter, W. Miller & D. Aaron, *The American Republic* (1959), 642.

servative wing took control and backed away from the liberal activism that had characterized the Roosevelt Court.

By the late 1940's, the strength of the Court's liberal wing was waning. As will be recalled, the Roosevelt Court had become increasingly divided on the subject of the proper role of the federal judiciary. At mid-decade, a five-vote coalition of moderate Justices was generally able to prevent the emergence of aggressive judicial liberal activism.

Subsequent appointments to the Bench by President Harry Truman then substantially enhanced the power of the Court's "less liberal" wing. In 1945, Roberts retired. Truman, in a fit of bi-partisanship, secured the open position for Harold H. Burton (1945–58), a Republican Senator who promptly affiliated with the Court's new "conservative" wing. In 1946, Chief Justice Stone, by then an economic moderate, died. Truman selected the more conservative Fred Vinson (1946–53) to replace him. Vinson, a former New Deal congressman and federal appellate judge, had been one of Truman's closest advisors in the first months of his presidency, and he continued to consult with Truman on policy matters after becoming Chief Justice. Vinson soon became the dominant member of the so-called "Vinson bloc" and the most powerful Justice of the Vinson Court.

Both Burton and Vinson were advocates of judicial restraint in the pre-1937 sense of the concept. That is, they were essentially Holmesian liberals, but they were definitely not activists. Their arrival made it far easier for the moderates to restrain any Supreme Court crusade for the social and economic underdog.

From 1946 to 1949, the Justices tended to divide along the lines shown in Table 19.

TABLE 19
Alignment of Justices, 1946–49

Left	Center	Right
Murphy		Jackson
Rutledge		Frankfurter
Douglas		Vinson
Black		Burton
		Reed

The seating of Burton and Vinson triggered an immediate shift to the right in the Court's voting patterns. In the October 1946 Term, for example, dissents by the most liberal Justices, Rutledge and Murphy, leaped to a level double that of the prior term.[3] The swing to the right was probably most pronounced in civil liberties cases, but it was detectable in economic cases as well.

The Vinson Court's economic conservatism was not, however, of the same vintage as that of the 1890's, 1920's, or 1930's. Foremost among the differences was that the role of constitutional censor of economic legislation was not reassumed. Indeed, the Holmesian principle of judicial restraint in such matters continued to dominate the Court's thinking.

Why, then, refer to the Vinson Court as conservative? The explanation is that the concepts of economic liberalism and conservatism had taken on new meanings after the constitutional revolution of 1937. Traditional economic conservatism—that is, constitutional activism on behalf of the rich—lost virtually all its support after 1937 and for the most part vanished from the United States judicial landscape. Henceforth, the policy of activism on behalf of the poor and the disadvantaged, which was endorsed by Justices Black and Douglas, came to characterize the liberal viewpoint. And the policy of judicial restraint became the hallmark of modern judicial conservatism. The Vinson Court was conservative in the post-1937 sense.

The Vinson Court's swing toward economic conservatism has been traced back as far as *United States v. United Mine Workers*,[4] which upheld an injunction against a UMW strike and fines against the union's president, John L. Lewis, and his union for breaches of that injunction.[5] The case marked a major departure from the pro-labor stance that had been characteristic of the Roosevelt Court. Even Black and Douglas deserted the liberal camp, leaving Murphy and Rutledge to dissent by themselves.

The *UMW* ruling typified the Vinson Court's particular brand of economic conservatism. The majority used legislative interpretation to achieve results consistent with the nation's prevailing anti-labor mood;

---

3. Murphy's dissent rate jumped from 9.2% to 23.0%. Rutledge's dissent rate rose from 14.9% to 28.9%. In contrast, Frankfurter's dissent rate went down slightly. *See* Galloway, *supra* note 1, this chapter, at 377.

4. 330 U.S. 258 (1947).

5. *See* Pritchett, *The Roosevelt Court*, 232–38. In 1948, Pritchett identified *United Mine Workers* as a turning point and an indicator that the liberal Roosevelt Court had given way to a more conservative Vinson Court. "[A]lready the temper of the Court is changing, and a swing to the right is apparent in several fields.... At the moment my own guess is that the Roosevelt Court came to an end on that Thursday in March 1947, when the John L. Lewis decision was handed down." *Id.*, xiv.

it did not erect constitutional barriers to nullify applicable labor statutes, as the pre-1937 Court was inclined to do.

Adamson v. California[6] provides a second illustration of the early Vinson Court's rejection of liberal activism. At issue in this conflict was whether the fifth amendment self-incrimination clause was binding on the States, but the broader, underlying issue was whether the entire Bill of Rights, with its many important protections for individual citizens, was applicable to the States. In a dissent that achieved landmark status for the ideas it introduced into judicial thinking, Justice Black, with concurrences by Douglas, Murphy, and Rutledge, pled eloquently for making the Bill of Rights applicable to the States, which would have triggered a constitutional revolution in criminal procedure. The conservatives closed ranks, however, and rejected the plea.

Once again, *Adamson* reflected a new conservatism. The Constitution was not invoked here to render a legislative measure void; rather, the majority simply declined to use the Constitution in an activist manner to nullify government action. *Adamson* further typified the post-1937 judicial situation in that its economically conservative effects resulted indirectly from the Court's attitude toward civil liberties rather than from favoritism for the rich.

In 1949, the Court's shift to the right became a rout. In the summer of that year, the liberal forces were decimated by the sudden deaths of Murphy and Rutledge.[7] To succeed them, Truman selected two moderately conservative Justices, Tom C. Clark (1949–67)[8] and Sherman Minton (1949–56).[9] Thus, the Court that presided during the Mc-

---

6. 332 U.S. 46 (1947).

7. The same summer, Justice Douglas was severely injured when his horse fell on him, crushing his ribs. Douglas missed most of the next term.

8. *See* 4 Friedman & Israel, *The Justices of the United States*, 2665–77. Clark, a former Texas lawyer and United States Attorney General had played a key role in the World War II Japanese relocation and the government's anti-subversive witchhunts. His appointment evoked strong opposition from liberals, who considered him anti-labor, anti-blacks, and anti-civil liberties. "As expected, Clark strengthened Vinson's position. In his first four years, the new justice almost always voted with his Chief. . . ." *Id.*, 2668. Clark "brought the fears of the Cold War to the Supreme Court and helped translate them into the law of the land." *Id.*, 2665. Harry Truman later said, "[Putting] Tom Clark [on the Supreme Court] was my biggest mistake. No question about it. . . . It's just that he's such a dumb son of a bitch. He's about the dumbest man I think I've ever run across." M. Miller, *Plain Speaking* (1984), 225–26.

9. *See* 4 Friedman & Israel, *The Justices of the United States*, 2699–2709. "[Minton's career] seemed to fall into two inconsistent parts: a liberal part as a member of the Senate and a conservative part as a member of the Court." *Id.*, 2708. The Minton

Carthy Era had its liberal wing reduced to two Justices, while its remaining seven members embraced a predominantly restrained, conservative outlook regarding the civil liberties issues that were suddenly of major national importance.

TABLE 20
Alignment of Justices, 1949–53

Left	Center	Right
Douglas	Frankfurter	Vinson
Black		Burton
		Clark
		Minton
		Reed
		Jackson

For the next four years, the conservatives had their way. Using their numerical superiority effectively, they outright dominated the Court. Vinson, the Bench's most powerful member and leader of a five-vote bloc that included Reed, Burton, Clark, and Minton, dissented only infrequently. In contrast, the number of dissents registered by Douglas and Black leaped to modern record levels. In the October 1952 Term, for example, Douglas dissented in 50% of the cases.

The leading case in the Court's continued move to the right was *Dennis v. United States*,[10] which upheld the conviction of 11 "first-string" leaders of the American Communist Party under the Smith Act. The statute prohibited advocacy of the doctrine that the government should be overthrown by force, and membership in any organization advocating that doctrine. The trial attracted enormous national attention during 1949. When the case reached the Supreme Court in 1951, the ma-

---

appointment was cheered by liberals who thought the former Indiana Senator, Seventh Circuit judge, and New Deal supporter would join the Black-Douglas wing. Instead, Minton joined Vinson's judicial-restraint group. "Rather than join the liberal bloc, he helped to strengthen the hand of Chief Justice Vinson and to create a five-man conservative bloc." *Id.*, 2703. "In the 1930's, Minton was a militant and outspoken New Dealer. Had he functioned as a Justice then, he would have been known as a liberal, for he would have tolerated efforts by government agencies to control economic affairs. In the 1950's, however, after the big issues had changed, he was regarded as one of the most conservative members of the Court. His point of view encouraged him to tolerate government restrictions on freedom of thought and other actions that alarmed civil libertarians." *Id.*, 2699.

10. 341 U.S. 494 (1951).

jority upheld all convictions, adopting a new constitutional test allowing convictions without a clear and present danger of imminent illegal action. This retreat on the free speech rights of dissidents and reformers typified the Vinson Court's conservatism and constitutional restraint.

For the country at the time, the central significance of the *Dennis* decision was its unmistakable signal that the Vinson Court did not intend to interfere with the burgeoning campaign against both real subversives and economic reformers who were also the victims of the reactionary tide. Thus McCarthy was left with an essentially free hand. The effect of McCarthy's ensuing assaults against advocates of assistance for the poor cannot be measured. Nevertheless, it seems clear in retrospect that the threat of being labelled and attacked as a communist or communist sympathizer deterred all but the most hardy from pressing for any major economic reforms.

14

The Warren Court (1953–1969)[1]

Over the course of the Supreme Court's second liberal era, however, the rule of "conservatism through restraint" was destined to be only temporary. In much the same manner that the 1906–20 "not quite progressive era" proved to be little more than a passing exception in a period of predominantly conservative activism on the Supreme Court, the Vinson approach to civil liberties and economics was soon superseded by the Warren Court's more liberal approach.

From 1953 to 1957, a renewed trend toward liberal activism appeared on the Court. This resurgence was made possible by what President Dwight D. Eisenhower later claimed were his two biggest "mistakes," the appointments of Earl Warren and William J. Brennan. In 1953, Chief Justice Vinson died. For his successor, Eisenhower chose the most liberal Chief Justice since Taney, Earl Warren (1953–69), California's progressive Republican governor.[2] After spending two terms

---

1. The best general discussion of the Warren Court is H. Schwartz, *Superchief* (1983). For other discussions of the Warren era, see A. Bickel, *Politics and the Warren Court* (1973); A. Cox, *The Warren Court* (1968); P. Kurland, *Politics, the Constitution, and the Warren Court* (1969).

2. A good account of Warren's career and philosophy of judging is E. White, *Earl Warren: A Public Life* (1982). Warren's identification with the common people developed very early in his life, in part as a result of his observations of employee mistreatment by the Southern Pacific Railroad. As Warren put it,

> My experience . . . in my railroad jobs was more meaningful because I was dealing with people as they worked for a gigantic corporation that dominated the economic and political life of the community. I saw that power exercised and the hardship that followed in its wake. I saw every man on the railroad not essential for the operation laid off without pay and without warning for weeks before the end of the fiscal year in order that the corporate stock might pay a higher dividend. I saw minority groups brought into the country for cheap labor paid a dollar a day for ten hours of work only to be fleeced out of much of that at the company store where they were obliged to trade. I helped carry men to the little room called the emergency hospital for amputation of an arm or leg that had been crushed because there were no safety applicances in the shops and yards to prevent such injuries. I knew of men who were fired for even considering a suit against the railroad for the injuries they had sustained. There was no compensation for them, and they

in the Court's ideological center, Warren moved into close alignment with Black and Douglas and remained there until his resignation in 1969. The liberal-activist wing was back up to three.

In 1954, Jackson died. Since his replacement, John Marshall Harlan (1955–71), was also a conservative, the succession did not change the Court's ideological alignment. Harlan, a former Wall Street lawyer, moved directly to the Court's far right in his first term and remained there throughout most of his tenure.[3]

Two years later, Minton retired, and Eisenhower appointed William J. Brennan (1956–1990), a former labor lawyer and liberal New Jersey state court judge, who brought a fourth vote to the Douglas, Black, and Warren wing.[4] Table 21 shows the line-up of Justices immediately after Brennan's arrival.

---

went through life as cripples. I witnessed crime and vice of all kinds countenanced by corrupt government.... The things I learned about monopolistic power, political dominance, corruption in government, and their effect on the people of a community were valuable lessons that would tend to shape my career....

E. Warren, *Memoirs* (1977), 30–31. Warren's political hero was Hiram Johnson, the leader of the California progressive movement who broke Southern Pacific's dominance over California politics. Warren considered himself a progressive throughout his career.

3. *See* 4 Friedman & Israel, *The Justices of the United States*, 2803–20. Harlan was a Justice of "conservative leaning" and "conservative philosophy." *Id.*, 2819, 2820. In the 1960's, he became known as the "conservative conscience to a highly active Court." *Id.*, 2803. "John Harlan had fashioned a grand career at the bar, squarely in the tradition of his great New York predecessors, Elihu Root, Grenville Clark, Emory Buckner and Arthur Ballantine.... If there was any lack at all in his preparation, it was probably the absence of direct exposure to the special problems of the less privileged sector of the community." *Id.*, 2805. "His law firm represented substantial financial interests, and a large part of Harlan's personal practice involved the defense of antitrust and other actions brought by the federal government. Sensitive from long experience to the effect of government economic regulation on the activities of corporations and businessmen, Harlan frequently voted to limit the impact of the antitrust laws and other federal regulatory statutes...." *Id.*, 2806. Harlan was a great Justice, who played a key role in the development of much of contemporary constitutional law.

4. *See* 2 Friedman & Israel, *The Justices of the United States*, 2849–65. Eisenhower picked Brennan as a bi-partisan gesture during the 1956 re-election campaign. Minton was a Catholic, and Ike instructed Attorney General Brownell to find a Catholic to replace him. Eisenhower later considered Brennan, like Warren, to be one of his biggest mistakes.

Soon known as the "bridge builder between the liberal and conservative Justices on the Court," *id.*, 2852, Brennan was nearer the center than Douglas, Black, and Warren, but his basic alignment with the liberals was observable from his first term. One of the

TABLE 21
Alignment of Justices, 1956–57

Left	Center	Right
Douglas	Clark[5]	Harlan
Black		Frankfurter
Warren		Burton
Brennan		Reed

Obviously, this Court was much more liberal than when a 7–2 conservative majority held sway under Vinson. The liberals needed only one more vote to become a majority. During the mid-1950's, they were frequently able to pick up the extra vote from Clark, Frankfurter, and, in scattered cases, other Justices.

From the start, the Warren Court continued the pattern set in 1937 and declined to act as constitutional censor of economic reform legislation.[6] As the majority stated a few years later, "We have returned to the original proposition that courts do not substitute their social and economic beliefs for the judgment of legislative bodies, who are elected to pass laws."[7] Conservative activism of the pre-1937 vintage, in short, remained out of the question. The real question was whether Warren and his supporters might adopt an activist, reforming brand of liberalism.

A shift away from conservative dominance became noticeable as early as the Court's October 1953 and 1954 Terms.[8] The big event of the day was *Brown v. Board of Education*,[9] the landmark school desegregation case that threw out the separate-but-equal doctrine and converted the equal protection clause into a powerful force for equality. *Brown*, of course, was one of the greatest victories ever won by racial minorities in the Supreme Court, and it is widely viewed as the start of the modern civil rights revolution. Warren played a crucial role in bringing a previously divided Court into unanimity on school deseg-

---

greatest Justices in the history of the Supreme Court, Brennan was the senior member of the Court's liberal opposition from 1975 to 1990.

5. Clark had been a member of the conservative wing during the Vinson era. When Warren joined the Court, Clark moved into a more moderate position. In later years, Clark continued to oscillate between moderate and conservative positions.

6. *See, e.g., Williamson v. Lee Optical Co.*, 348 U.S. 483 (1955).

7. *Ferguson v. Skrupa*, 372 U.S. 726, 730 (1963).

8. *See* Galloway, *The Early Years of the Warren Court: Emergence of Judicial Liberalism (1953-1957)*, 18 Santa Clara L. Rev. 609, 612–16 (1978).

9. 347 U.S. 483 (1954).

regation; his performance impressed his fellow Justices greatly and marked a major first step in his development as the "Superchief."

During the October 1955 and 1956 Terms, liberal activism was definitely on the rise. For example, the landmark 1956 case *Griffin v. Illinois*[10] held that indigent criminal defendants are entitled to a free trial transcript for purposes of appeal. "There can be no equal justice," the Court stated, "where the kind of trial a man gets depends on the amount of money he has."[11] *Griffin* was the first in a long series of cases in which the Court expanded the rights of indigent criminal defendants under the equal protection and due process clauses of the fourteenth amendment. The series is widely recognized as a prime indicator of the Warren Court's egalitarianism and liberal activism on behalf of the poor.[12]

The Warren Court of the mid-1950's also made a major effort to roll back the political repression characteristic of the times. The string of rulings in this regard is too long to discuss in detail, but its leading cases deserve brief mention. In *Pennsylvania v. Nelson*,[13] the Court held that federal statutes, including the Smith Act, occupied the field of subversion against the United States and nullified all state laws on the subject. In *Watkins v. United States*,[14] the majority shook a stick at the House Un-American Activities Committee (HUAC), stating that Congress has no authority to investigate for purposes of punishment or to publish for purposes of mere exposure. That same day, in *Yates v. United States*,[15] the Court drastically restricted the Smith Act by construing it to prohibit only incitement of "action" to overthrow the government, not advocacy of "abstract ideas." *Yates* reversed the convictions of the "second-string" leaders of the United States Communist Party and brought the Justice Department's prosecutions of communists to a virtual halt. The pattern of *Nelson, Watkins*, and *Yates* was manifest in a series of additional decisions attempting to establish a basically open society in which economic and political alternatives could be discussed and advocated without fear of retribution.[16]

---

10. 351 U.S. 12 (1956).
11. *Id.*, 19.
12. *See, e.g.*, Cox, *The Warren Court*, 7.
13. 350 U.S. 497 (1956).
14. 354 U.S. 178 (1957).
15. 354 U.S. 298 (1957).
16. These cases include *Sweezy v. New Hampshire*, 354 U.S. 234 (1957) (restricting

The Court's efforts to turn back the repressive trends of the 1950's gave rise to an outburst of hostile public reaction.[17] The press was full of criticism. "Impeach Earl Warren" became a widely known slogan advanced by the newly formed John Birch Society. Legislation was introduced to curb the power of the Court.[18] The assembled chief justices of the state supreme courts passed a resolution opposing liberal activism on the Supreme Court. In response to the public furor, the Court quietly withdrew from its liberal-activist posture. The cross-over members of the moderate and conservative ranks moved back to the right and increasingly deprived the liberals of their needed fifth vote. This relative quiescence was to prevail until 1961.[19]

Additional changes in Court personnel made toward the end of the 1950's helped sustain the Bench's withdrawal from liberal activism. In 1957, the then conservative Reed retired. He was succeeded by Charles E. Whittaker (1957–62), a corporate lawyer from St. Louis. "Whittaker immediately aligned himself with the conservative justices on the Court."[20] He remained a member of that bloc throughout his brief tenure and, in fact, posted the Court's most conservative voting record during his final term. Next Burton retired in 1958. He was succeeded by Potter Stewart (1958–81), a Cincinnati Republican, Sixth Circuit judge, and moderate conservative.[21]

The retreat that characterized the Warren Court's 1958 to 1961 middle period is reflected in a wide range of decisions. Two 1958 rulings

---

state investigating committees); *Jencks v. United States*, 353 U.S. 657 (1957) (allowing access to FBI files to discover information provided by informers); *Konigsberg v. State Bar*, 353 U.S. 252 (1957) (restricting denial of bar membership to alleged subversives); *Schware v. Board of Bar Examiners*, 353 U.S. 232 (1957) (same); *Slochower v. Board of Educ.*, 350 U.S. 551 (1956) (restricting grounds for denial of municipal employment).

17. This outburst was described by Professor Alpheus Mason as follows: "Dissenting Justices and constitutional lawyers are outspoken in protest; members of Congress are stunned though not silenced. Not since 1937 when F.D.R. declared war on the Nine Old Men, has judicial authority been so roundly criticized. One hears again the familiar echo: 'Curb that Court before it destroys the nation.' Bring the Justices down from 'the pedestal of fetish and deal with them as men and not supermen.' " Mason, *The Supreme Court from Taft to Warren*, 4.

18. *See* W. Murphy, *Congress and the Court* (1962); C. Pritchett, *Congress Versus the Supreme Court 1957–1960* (1961).

19. *See* Galloway, *The Second Period of the Warren Court: The Liberal Trend Abates (1957–1961)*, 19 Santa Clara L. Rev. 947 (1979).

20. 4 Friedman & Israel, *The Justices of the United States*, 2896.

21. *See* Galloway, *Potter Stewart: Just a Lawyer*, 25 Santa Clara L. Rev. 523 (1985).

upheld the dismissal of employees for refusal to answer questions regarding alleged communist activity.[22] In 1959, the Court upheld contempt of Congress convictions for refusal to answer questions regarding communist activity[23] and for refusal to produce a guest list for an alleged communist-front summer camp.[24] Again, in 1960, the Court sustained the discharge of a social worker for refusing to answer questions before the House Un-American Activities Committee.[25] In short, as political scientist Jonathan Casper stated, "The period of 1958–1961 saw the Court step back from much of the doctrine it had appeared to be developing in the 1956–1957 period."[26]

History remembers, however, that the Court soon stepped forward again. During the early 1960's, two events occurred that made possible the emergence of the aggressive liberal judicial activism that has come to be known as the Warren Court's definitive characteristic. First, the nation at large shifted toward political liberalism. Manifestations of this trend included the election and presidency of John Fitzgerald Kennedy, the Civil Rights Movement, and Lyndon Johnson's Great Society programs (for example, the 1964 Civil Rights Act and Economic Development Act). Second, changes in Court personnel gave the liberal activists a five-vote majority that remained unbroken until 1969. As a result of these two developments, the Supreme Court, for the first time since its inception, became the active champion of the poor, not only resisting efforts to exploit the poor, but also initiating new programs for their benefit.[27]

The Warren Court's more conservative middle period ended in 1962 when Frankfurter retired and was replaced by Arthur Goldberg (1962–65),[28] a former counsel for the United Steelworkers and AFL-CIO. Goldberg provided the activist wing with the dependable additional vote needed for a consistent majority.[29] In addition, that same year, By-

---

22. *Lerner v. Casey*, 357 U.S. 468 (1958); *Beilan v. Board of Pub. Educ.*, 357 U.S. 299 (1958).

23. *Barenblatt v. United States*, 360 U.S. 109 (1959).

24. *Uphaus v. Wyman*, 360 U.S. 72 (1959).

25. *Nelson v. City of Los Angeles*, 362 U.S. 1 (1960).

26. J. Casper, *The Politics of Civil Liberties* (1972), 75.

27. *See* Galloway, *The Third Period of the Warren Court: Liberal Dominance (1962–1969)*, 20 Santa Clara L. Rev. 773 (1980).

28. Goldberg was "one of the most activist-liberal judges ever to occupy a seat on the Court." Casper, *The Politics of Civil Liberties*, 80.

29. The Goldberg appointment also brought the Court to the most liberal posture since its inception in 1790, surpassing the previous high point that had been set by the Black, Douglas, Murphy, Rutledge Court of the mid-1940's.

ron R. White (1962–present), a moderate conservative with liberal leanings in civil rights matters, replaced the conservative Charles E. Whittaker. Next, in 1965, Goldberg resigned to become Ambassador to the United Nations and was replaced by another liberal, Abe Fortas (1965–69).[30] Finally, in 1967, the moderate conservative Clark was succeeded by Thurgood Marshall (1967–present), a liberal who had been lead counsel in many major civil rights cases, including *Brown v. Board of Education*.[31]

Thus, by 1967, the Court had attained another unprecedented historic plateau with six liberals, two moderates, and one conservative.[32] The line-up looked like this.

TABLE 22
Alignment of Justices, 1967–69

Left	Center	Right
Douglas	White	Harlan
Warren	Stewart	
Brennan		
Marshall		
Fortas		
Black		

Numerous cases illustrate the Warren Court's willingness to assist

---

30. *See* B. Murphy, *Abe Fortas: The Rise and Ruin of a Supreme Court Justice* (1989). Fortas was a New Dealer who had been William O. Douglas' protege at Yale Law School and later at the SEC. He was counsel for petitioner in the great case *Gideon v. Wainwright*, 372 U.S. 335 (1963). He was also President Johnson's closest political advisor, and he continued to play that role during his service on the Court.

31. 347 U.S. 483 (1954). *See* 4 Friedman & Israel, *The Justices of the United States*, 3063–92. Marshall, who had labored for "a quarter century as the nation's most prominent civil rights lawyer," *id.*, 3063–64, was chief counsel for the NAACP Legal Defense Fund from 1938 to 1961. John F. Kennedy appointed him to a position as a federal appellate judge on the Second Circuit, and Lyndon Johnson made him United States Solicitor General. At the time of his appointment it was expected that "Marshall would join the Court's 'activist' and 'liberal' wing. He would favor the individual against the state, the weak and disabled against the strong, the federal government against the states, the regulators against the regulated. He would exalt the values of equality and subordinate the values of property." *Id.*, 3063. All these expectations proved accurate. Marshall has been a liberal throughout his tenure and remains a member of the Court's liberal opposition at the time of this writing.

32. Actually Black shifted into a relatively moderate position during the 1966–71 period, so his placement in the liberal wing is subject to some dispute. Even if Black is counted as a moderate, however, the liberal-activists had an absolute five-vote majority.

the poor in their economic and social struggles. First, consider the core area of poverty law, government benefit programs. According to prior law, statutorily mandated financial assistance to the needy, such as old-age benefits, aid to the blind, and aid to families with dependent children, were "privileges" that the government was not compelled to grant and could therefore cut off without warning or justification. The Warren Court, in a move typical of its activist phase, rejected the right-privilege distinction and held that persons who qualify for these programs acquire a legally protected "property" interest in their benefits that cannot be taken away without complying with the procedural requirements of the due process clauses.[33]

In general, welfare recipients received sympathetic treatment from the Warren Court. Although the number of welfare cases at bar was small, those that were decided usually went in favor of the recipients.[34] Moreover, toward the end of the decade, the Court appeared to be moving toward formal recognition of the principle that economic subsistence benefits are a fundamental right and that poverty is a suspect classification, thus subjecting denials of such benefits to strict judicial scrutiny.[35] Encouraged by the Warren Court's decisions, legal services attorneys developed a bustling field of activity known as welfare reform litigation and initiated many successful suits to repair deficiencies in the public welfare system.

Another line of rulings that illustrate the Warren Court's role as protector of the poor concerned publicly financed assistance for indigent

---

33. *E.g., Sniadach v. Family Finance Corp.*, 395 U.S. 337 (1969) (holding that pretrial garnishment without a prior hearing violates due process). Actually, the most important case in the line, *Goldberg v. Kelly*, 397 U.S. 254 (1970), came down during the first term of the Burger Court, but it was a "Warren Court case" in that the majority was made up of Warren Court liberals, and Chief Justice Burger dissented. *See* Reich, *The New Property*, 73 Yale L.J. 733 (1969).

34. *E.g., Shapiro v. Thompson*, 394 U.S. 618 (1969) (public assistance residency requirement held unconstitutional); *King v. Smith*, 392 U.S. 309 (1968) (denial of public assistance based on presence of "man assuming role of spouse" held illegal). The reason few welfare cases were decided by the Warren Court is that the legal assistance program initiated by the Economic Development Act of 1964 was just getting underway in the late 1960's, and welfare reform cases were slow in working their way through the lower courts.

35. Government action that is subject to strict scrutiny is presumptively unconstitutional and must be struck down unless the government proves that its action is necessary to further a compelling government interest. *Shapiro v. Thompson*, 394 U.S. 618 (1969), and *Hunter v. Erickson*, 393 U.S. 385 (1969), are usually cited as the cases which came closest to holding that denials of welfare benefits are subject to strict scrutiny.

criminal defendants.[36] These cases were based on the recognition that, because they could not afford to pay the requisite fees, poor people were often unable to obtain fair trials. The seminal case in this development, *Griffin v. Illinois*,[37] has already been mentioned.[38] Among the many progeny of *Griffin*, the most famous was *Douglas v. California*,[39] which held that States must provide free appellate counsel for indigent defendants. By the end of Warren's tenure, the so-called *Griffin-Douglas* rule had generated a substantial body of decisions implementing the general concept that the kind of trial an individual receives should not depend on the amount of money he has.

The Warren Court's activism on behalf of the poor was also evident in *Gideon v. Wainwright*,[40] which held that indigent defendants are entitled under the sixth amendment, to free court-appointed attorneys in felony trials. The ruling, obviously, was a direct attempt to aid the poor and revealed a willingness to move into new areas and create new legal rules for the protection of the poor.

A third illustration of the Warren Court's empathy with the poor is the liberal and activist stance taken in civil rights litigation. In some instances, the Court directly and explicitly attempted to insure that poor persons are not deprived of important rights because of their poverty. For example, *Harper v. Virginia Board of Elections*[41] held that the right to vote may not be conditioned upon the payment of a poll tax since such a tax would deter indigent persons from exercising the franchise.

In other instances, the Warren Court's assistance to the poor was more indirect, though, in the long run, perhaps of greater importance. For example, in response to the needs of citizens who suffered economic disadvantage as a result of racial and ethnic discrimination, the Warren Court developed new law on its own initiative and also broadly

---

36. A more famous series of Warren Court decisions increased the procedural protections of all criminal defendants, rich and poor alike. Since poverty is the great breeder of crime, these cases tended to assist the poor more than the rich. The discussion here, however, focuses on the narrower line of cases that are concerned specifically with impoverished defendants.

37. 351 U.S. 12 (1956).

38. *See supra* p. 140.

39. 372 U.S. 353 (1963).

40. 372 U.S. 335 (1963). For a detailed account of this famous case, see A. Lewis, *Gideon's Trumpet* (1964). The story was also made into a video with Henry Fonda playing Clarence Earl Gideon.

41. 383 U.S. 663 (1966).

construed the power of Congress to ban discrimination.[42] The classic instance of the Justices' taking the initiative was *Brown v. Board of Education*,[43] which overturned the separate but equal doctrine that had been dominant in educational institutions since the 1890's.

Finally, the Warren Court accorded Congress vast and unprecedented powers to prohibit private racial discrimination. During the 1960's, the majority upheld Congress' authority, under the commerce clause, to enact the Civil Rights Act of 1964, which prohibited racial discrimination in employment, housing, and public accommodations.[44] And, in a striking move, the Court resurrected the long dead Civil Rights Act of 1866, holding that Congress has power under the thirteenth amendment to prohibit private discrimination.[45] Armed with these decisions, civil rights advocates proceeded with intense litigation on behalf of minorities, particularly in the fields of employment and education.[46]

Overall, the Justices serving for most of the 1960's reflected in their thinking a more aggressive form of economic liberalism than had ever previously occurred in United States Supreme Court history. Prior to 1937, economic liberalism on the Supreme Court generally meant only a willingness to allow other branches of government to take action on behalf of the financially disadvantaged. This outlook left little room for positive effort by the Justices to advance the interests of the poor. Indeed, many of the earlier "liberal" jurists were politically and economically conservative in their personal viewpoints and exerted a liberal influence only because of their commitment to judicial restraint.[47] Conversely, judicial activism prior to 1937 was associated with economic conservatism and took the form of Justices' voting to nullify economic reform legislation.

After 1937, the Court's liberals embraced the policy of judicial activism and the conservatives took the cause of restraint.[48] From 1962 to

---

42. *See* Cox, *The Warren Court*, 24–70.

43. 347 U.S. 483 (1954).

44. *E.g., Katzenbach v. McClung*, 379 U.S. 294 (1964); *Heart of Atlanta Motel v. United States*, 379 U.S. 241 (1964).

45. *Jones v. Alfred H. Mayer Co.*, 392 U.S. 409 (1968).

46. Another area in which the Warren Court's economic liberalism was evident was antitrust, where the password became "the government always wins." *United States v. Von's Grocery Co.*, 384 U.S. 270, 301 (Stewart, J., dissenting).

47. The classic examples were Holmes and Stone.

48. The new pattern was strikingly illustrated by Felix Frankfurter, who presents a reversed image of Holmes and Stone. Frankfurter, an individual with deeply liberal

1969, the liberal activists had their period of greatest dominance while viewing themselves as the protectors of the poor rather than the rich. And for the first time in the nation's history, the Court majority began to exercise initiative on behalf of the poor.

---

personal convictions, became a Warren Court "conservative" due to his commitment to judicial restraint.

Part Six

*The Third Conservative Era
(1969–Present)*

15

The Burger Court (1969–1986)[1]

As the 1960's waned, the political mood of the American voter again shifted, this time sharply to the right, and the nation polarized. The liberalism of the early 1960's had been sustained by a wave of idealism. The Kennedy administration—with its youth, vigor, and intelligence—raised hopes that major socio-economic reform could be accomplished and fostered illusions that a new period of harmony and justice was dawning. Reformers believed that "we shall overcome" racial discrimination, poverty, and the competitive dog-eat-dog values of the Adam Smith model of capitalism. Idealism was particularly strong among the young, who felt that their mass demonstrations could help put an end to the unjust features of the established order.

In the latter half of the sixties, the wave ebbed. Innocence was lost. The freedom rides and sit-ins produced some worthwhile results, but they also precipitated an intense backlash of bigotry and repression. The same political leaders who spoke of a Great Society let the nation fall deeper and deeper into the unpopular Vietnam War that mocked the reformers' idealism and led to bitter disillusionment. Clearly, the roots of the systemic injustice the "movement" was attempting to change were deeper and more intractable than many had expected. The encounter with unyielding resistance gave rise to anger on the part of many reformers.

As it became increasingly apparent the establishment was not going to change its practices, anger burst into violence. Riots rocked ghettoes across the nation. Reformers became revolutionaries. Nonviolence yielded to terror tactics. This, in turn, intensified the backlash and gave

---

1. *See* H. Schwartz, *The Burger Years* (1987). A widely read, provocative, oft-criticized account of the 1969–76 period is B. Woodward & S. Armstrong, *The Brethren* (1979). *See also* V. Blasi, *The Burger Court: The Counterrevolution That Wasn't* (1983); Galloway, *The Burger Court (1969–1986)*, 27 Santa Clara L. Rev. 31 (1987); Galloway, *The First Decade of the Burger Court: Conservative Dominance (1969–1979)*, 21 Santa Clara L. Rev. 891 (1981).

rise to violent counterattacks on demonstrators at Cicero, Kent State, and the tumultuous 1968 Chicago Democratic Convention.

The event that, more than any other, turned the tide against the spirit of reform and brought slightly more than 30 years of judicial liberalism to a close was Richard Nixon's 1968 election to the White House. The narrow margin of Nixon's victory over liberal Vice President Hubert Humphrey suggests that the nation's political mood had not swung dramatically to the right before late 1968. When Nixon became President, however, the defeat of the reform movement became evident. His administration quickly applied its great skill in the use of the communications media to mobilize the backlash and encourage the repressive side of the "silent majority." Law and order were now the passwords,[2] and further reform efforts were to be suppressed. These developments were epitomized by the Huston Plan[3] and the massive lock-up of anti-war marchers in Washington, D.C. in 1969.[4]

A. The Supreme Court Swings to the Right (1969–1972)

The swing to the right in the nation at large was followed by one of the most dramatic short-term changes of judicial personnel in the history of the United States Supreme Court.[5] Within a stretch of approximately 30 months between the summer of 1969 and early 1972, the Court changed from a configuration of six liberals, two moderates, and one conservative[6] to a configuration of three liberals, two moderates, and four conservatives. In June 1969, the liberal activists enjoyed

---

2. The law and order standard was applied by the Nixon administration only to its opponents, not to its own members, as the Watergate scandal later revealed.

3. The Huston Plan was a blueprint drawn up by a member of the Nixon administration calling for a systematic assault by agencies of the federal government against dissidents. The plan contemplated large-scale domestic surveillance, infiltration of dissident groups, and suppression of protests.

4. The Nixon repression also brought to an end the "Aquarian Age," the shortest period of American history to date. This age of peace, love, and feeling groovy lasted approximately one year, from the 1968 Woodstock rock concert to the 1969 Altamont concert.

5. Other major short-term changes on the Court include the seating of Barbour and Taney in 1837; the appointments of Fuller (1888) and Brewer (1890); the Harding appointments of the early 1920's; the Roosevelt appointments following the constitutional revolution of 1937; the 1949 replacement of Murphy and Rutledge by Clark and Minton, and the 1962 Frankfurter-Goldberg succession. None of these was more decisive than the shift that occurred in the 1969–72 period.

6. If Black is counted as a moderate because of his shift to the right in the 1966–71 period, the split was 5–3–1 rather than 6–2–1.

an unbeatable six-vote majority.[7] By January 7, 1972, it was difficult for the liberals to win any controversial case.

The transition from the liberalism of the Warren era to the conservatism of the Burger era took place with unusual speed. Normally, the Supreme Court lags behind the elective branches. The Court, representing the attitudes of the recent past, provides a longitudinal check and balance on Congress and the President, who in turn represent the present mood of the electorate. The national swing to the right that came to fruition in 1968, however, was transmitted to the Court with highly abnormal, almost shocking suddenness.

The change began in 1968, when liberal judicial strategists committed a monumental blunder in attempting to pack the Court before the end of Lyndon Johnson's presidency.[8] By then, the Democratic leadership had collapsed under its own mistakes in conducting the Vietnam War. The threat of a Nixon victory in the November election was apparent. Chief Justice Warren despised Nixon and correctly surmised that, given the chance, Nixon would destroy the Court as an activist instrument for social reform.[9]

Applying a tactic the conservatives had used well in 1801, the liberals devised a plan to secure their dominance on the future Court. Earl Warren would retire. President Johnson would promote Associate Justice Abe Fortas to Chief Justice. Another liberal would be selected to take Fortas' seat. After Warren announced his retirement, however, a problem arose. Fortas was attacked during his confirmation hearings for accepting a substantial honorarium while on the Court. Then, after Fortas had requested that the nomination be withdrawn, he was accused of accepting a $20,000 a year retainer from Lewis Wolfson, a financier who was being investigated for securities fraud. Under pressure, Fortas resigned. Thus, instead of a relatively young liberal Chief Justice, plus five liberal Associates, Nixon inherited a Court with a lame duck Chief Justice, an open seat, and only four liberals.

---

7. This was the most liberal configuration in Supreme Court history to date. The Roosevelt Court had an eight-vote liberal wing in constitutional cases involving economic issues, but only four members were crusading activists of the 1960's stripe.

8. *See* H. Schwartz, *Superchief* (1983), 680–83, 720–22, for a more detailed account of these events.

9. For more details on Warren's hatred for Nixon, see *id.*, 21, 336–37. According to Earl Warren, Jr., Warren "just detested Richard Nixon with an abiding passion." *Id.*, 21. The feud went back to the 1952 Republican Convention, when Nixon tried to persuade delegates committed to Warren's favorite-son candidacy to abandon Warren and support Eisenhower. *Id.*

Like William Howard Taft and Franklin Delano Roosevelt, Richard Milhouse Nixon knew the utility of having a Supreme Court that saw things his way. Indeed, he had campaigned against the Warren Court nearly as much as against Humphrey. Therefore, Nixon set out to find a new Chief and Associate Justice who shared his views regarding the nature of the Supreme Court and the meaning of the Constitution.[10] Accordingly, Nixon appointed two conservative federal appellate judges and former corporate lawyers to the Bench, Chief Justice Warren E. Burger (1969–86)[11] and Associate Justice Harry A. Blackmun (1970–present).[12] The pair's initial views were so closely aligned that they soon became known, in reference to their common home State, as the "Minnesota Twins." Thus, scarcely a year after Nixon took office, he had already managed to alter the Court's balance of power dramatically.

President Nixon, as mentioned above, said he would choose Justices who shared his views on constitutional adjudication. What were his views on the rich-poor issue? The basic concept was that the Court should be restrained rather than activist and that it should not exercise so much initiative in attempting to rectify economic inequality. In his campaign, Nixon pledged "to nominate to the Supreme Court individuals who shared my judicial philosophy, which is basically a conservative philosophy."[13]

This plan for the judiciary was but one component of Nixon's general political program. Nixon saw his role in history—at least in the

---

10. The substance of these views will be discussed below.

11. For a brief account of Burger's career, see 4 Friedman & Israel, *The Justices of the United States*, 3111–42. Burger had practiced law for more than 20 years with a corporate law firm in St. Paul and then, after three years with the Eisenhower Justice Department, become a member of the conservative wing of the Court of Appeals for the D.C. Circuit. Burger posted the most conservative voting record on the Court during his first term and later settled into the position of the Court's second most conservative Justice behind William H. Rehnquist.

12. *See* 5 Friedman & Israel, *The Justices of the United States*, 3–21. Nixon chose Blackmun because of his reputation as a conservative judge on the Court of Appeals for the Eighth Circuit and because Blackmun seemed likely to provide his old friend Burger a virtual proxy vote. Blackmun had lived in the same St. Paul neighborhood as Burger, gone to the same Sunday school, and been best man at Burger's wedding. Although not as conservative as Burger, Blackmun was a core conservative throughout the early 1970's with the possible exception of the October 1974 Term, when he shifted toward a moderate position. Later, beginning in 1977, Blackmun shifted away from his conservative Brethren, crossed over the Court's statistical center, and became the Court's third most liberal member.

13. R. Nixon, *Public Papers of the President* (1972), 1055.

realm of domestic politics—as destroyer of the New Deal. For too long, he believed, the federal government had extended its economic control over the people and, especially, the business corporations of the nation. Now, by forging a political coalition out of the silent majority who still believed in free enterprise and the traditional moral order, Nixon would reverse history and dismantle the welfare state.[14]

The conservative effect of Nixon's Supreme Court appointments was felt immediately. Already during the October 1969 Term, the first post-Warren term, voting statistics showed a shift to the right,[15] and the Burger Court began its retreat from the leading outposts of Warren Court liberal activism. Indeed, the Court gave prompt notice in its decisions that the Bench's egalitarian revolution was over.

The leading ideas of then emerging egalitarian legal theory were that welfare assistance is a fundamental right, that poverty is a legally suspect classification,[16] and that legislation discriminating against welfare recipients is therefore subject to strict strutiny as regards its constitutionality. The Burger Court rejected these ideas. The most important conservative victory in the October 1969 Term was *Dandridge v. Williams*,[17] the landmark case upholding a "maximum grant" limit on Aid to Families with Dependent Children and rejecting the claim that subsistence welfare benefits are a fundamental right. On the same day in 1970, *Rosado v. Wyman*[18] sustained a statute imposing "percentage reductions" of welfare grants below state-determined need. *Dandridge* and *Rosado* were watershed cases indicating that a chill had descended on the area of welfare reform through constitutional litigation.

Blackmun's 1970 arrival consolidated a pattern of conservative dominance that lasted through most of the decade. In the October 1970 Term, Blackmun was on the Court's far right statistically. He agreed

---

14. One of the most striking manifestations of this program was Nixon's attempt to weaken the legal services and community action programs that had been the centerpieces of President Johnson's war on poverty. For example, Nixon appointed as director of the Office of Economic Opportunity Howard Phillips, an ardent opponent of the war on poverty. The purpose of the appointment was to destroy the OEO, not to administer it.

15. *See* Galloway, *The First Decade of the Burger Court: Conservative Dominance (1969–1979)*, 21 Santa Clara L. Rev. 891, 893–97 (1981).

16. A suspect classification is a constitutionally disfavored classification that is subject to strict scrutiny rather than the deferential rational basis test that usually applies in equal protection cases. Race is the most suspect of all classifications. Sex is a "semi-suspect" classification.

17. 397 U.S. 471 (1970).

18. 397 U.S. 397 (1970).

with Burger in 95.3% of the cases, solidifying the "Minnesota Twins" nickname. Chief Justice Burger's dissent rate went from the *highest* on the Court the prior term to the *lowest* in the October 1970 Term, while Douglas' dissent rate skied to 41.3%, his highest since the first term of the Warren era.

Any remaining doubt about the Nixon Court's determination to retrench in the area of poverty law was removed in 1971, when *James v. Valtierra*[19] upheld a California constitutional provision requiring approval by local referendum before installation of low rent housing within a community. Here was clear discrimination against the poor. No referenda were required for normal housing; they were only mandated for housing for the poor. Applying the deferential rational basis test, the Court found this type of discrimination permissible, inflicting a major defeat on low-income persons in their efforts to live outside ghettoes.[20]

Continuing conservative dominance during the October 1971 Term, third of the Burger era, is illustrated by Douglas' 43.8% dissent rate and by a series of conservative victories in cases having important economic effects. *Lindsay v. Normet*,[21] for example, held that housing is not a fundamental right for purposes of equal protection analysis. Even more important, the landmark cases *Board of Regents v. Roth*[22] and *Perry v. Sinderman*[23] undercut the foundations of the recent procedural due process revolution by holding that government benefits, no matter how important, are not "property" within the meaning of procedural due process unless the law creating them confers an "entitlement" to receive the benefits.

The waning of liberal activism proceeded a step further when Justices Black and Harlan retired in September 1971. To replace Black, Nixon appointed Lewis F. Powell, Jr. (1972–87), a conservative corporate attorney from Richmond, Virginia.[24] Powell promptly lined up

---

19. 402 U.S. 137 (1971).

20. Another illustrative 1971 conservative victory that cut back protections both for the poor and for civil liberty was *Wyman v. James*, 400 U.S. 309 (1971), which held that required home visits do not violate the privacy rights of welfare recipients.

21. 405 U.S. 56 (1972).

22. 408 U.S. 564 (1972).

23. 408 U.S. 593 (1972).

24. *See* 5 Friedman & Israel, *The Justices of the United States*, 63–83. Powell was a pillar of the legal establishment, a former President of the American Bar Association, and a member of the boards of directors of a dozen major corporations. "When Justice Powell woke up in his sixty-fourth year a Justice of the Supreme Court, he remained

near the Court's far right close to Burger. To replace Harlan, Nixon chose William H. Rehnquist (1972–present), a conservative former Phoenix attorney, Goldwater Republican, and point man for the Nixon-Mitchell Justice Department.[25] Rehnquist immediately established himself on the Court's far right beyond even Chief Justice Burger. Table 23 shows the Court's line-up after the seating of Powell and Rehnquist.

TABLE 23
Alignment of Justices, 1972–75

Left	Center	Right
Douglas	Stewart	Rehnquist
Brennan	White	Burger
Marshall		Powell
		Blackmun

Clearly the days of liberal dominance were over.

The Powell and Rehnquist appointments completed the swing to the right that characterized the first phase of the Burger Court and initiated a second, more conservative period in which liberal activism faded rapidly.

B. *The Nixon Court: Conservative Dominance (1972–1977)*

The seating of Powell and Rehnquist in January 1972 marked the

---

very much the lawyer who for thirty-five years had gone to bed defending the interests of many of America's largest corporations." *Id.*, 79. Powell considers himself a conservative, promptly became one of the Court's core conservatives, and remained a member of the conservative wing throughout his tenure, with the possible exception of the October 1977 and 1986 Terms, when he voted in a more moderate fashion. Powell was especially close to Burger over the years, often agreeing with him in more than 90% of the cases. In the 1980's, Powell became widely known as the Court's "man in the middle," but he was statistically far right of center throughout that period.

25. *See* 5 Friedman & Israel, *The Justices of the United States*, 109–31. Rehnquist's conservatism is axiomatic. "William Hubbs Rehnquist has been, from the first dawning of his political awareness, a forceful, outspoken conservative." R. Kluger, *Simple Justice* (1975), 608 n.*. At Stanford Law School, where he was first in his class, "Bill was the school conservative. . . . He was so far-out politically that he was something of a joke." *Id.*, 608–09 n.*. "As I knew him, he was a reactionary," says Donald Trautman, Felix Frankfurter's clerk during the October 1952 Term, when Rehnquist clerked for Justice Robert Jackson. *Id.*, 608 n.*. Rehnquist posted the most conservative voting record every term from his arrival to the time of this writing except the October 1977 Term, when he was arguably ousted by Sandra Day O'Connor. He is the most conservative Justice since McReynolds' 1941 retirement.

start of five years in which the Court was dominated by the four Nixonians, Burger, Blackmun, Powell, and Rehnquist. This was the heyday of the "Nixon Court," and it witnessed probably the most conservative series of cases since the Court's attack on the New Deal in the mid-1930's.[26] The Nixonians usually picked up the extra votes they needed from White and Stewart, who were right of center during those years.[27]

Naturally, the liberals were distraught. In the October 1972 Term, Douglas' dissent rate leaped to 50.7%, a record for him and the highest dissent rate of any Justice since 1795. Douglas and Rehnquist disagreed in 92 out of 139 cases, a 66.2% disagreement rate that was also the highest since the 1790's. Brennan and Marshall posted dissent rates of 34.8% and 32.6% respectively, personal records for both.

The case that best symbolizes the Nixon Court's retreat on the rich-poor issue from the liberalism of the 1960's is *San Antonio Independent School District v. Rodriguez*,[28] the widely publicized and debated school finance case. The controversy involved a challenge to Texas' system for financing public education which, because it was based in large part on property taxes, had given rise to extreme differences in the amount of money available per child in rich and poor districts. Again, the Nixon Court made it clear that the days of liberal activism on behalf of the poor were over. Since in the view of Powell, Burger, Blackmun, Rehnquist, and Stewart, the Texas school financing system was not without some rational foundation, it was constitutional.[29] The decision helped perpetuate the cycle of poverty by insuring that children in poor districts receive less educational support than children in rich districts. Under Warren, the decision would almost certainly have gone the other way. Indeed, four of the five Warren Court holdovers—Douglas, Brennan, Marshall, and White—dissented.[30]

---

26. An argument could be made that the decisions of the Vinson Court during the McCarthy Era were more conservative.

27. White had a surprisingly conservative voting record in the early 1970's. For example, he disagreed with Douglas in 57.2% of the cases in the 1972 Term.

28. 411 U.S. 1 (1973).

29. In reaching the conclusion that the rational basis test was controlling rather than the strict scrutiny test, the Court made two additional conservative decisions: (1) that the right to equal educational opportunity is not a fundamental right; and (2) that district wealth classifications are not suspect.

30. The Court of the early 1970's did not entirely abandon the concept that poverty is an inadequate basis for denying important rights. *See, e.g., Bullock v. Carter*, 405 U.S. 134 (1972) (impoverished candidates for office need not pay filing fee); *Tate v. Short*, 401 U.S. 395 (1971) (persons may not be jailed simply because they are too poor to pay criminal fines).

Then, in 1974, the Court signalled the end of the egalitarian revolution on behalf of indigent criminal defendants. That year, in *Ross v. Moffitt*,[31] the Court held that the government need not assign attorneys to indigent criminal defendants to help prepare petitions for discretionary review of their convictions in either state or federal supreme courts. *Ross* cut back the reigning *Griffin-Douglas* rule[32] by holding that the Constitution requires only that indigents be provided an adequate opportunity for a fair adjudication. If this standard is met, the majority concluded, the Warren Court's principle that the kind of justice a person receives should not depend on the amount of money he has is inapplicable.[33]

The following year, the Court's liberal wing suffered still another setback when Justice Douglas, the Court's most liberal member for more than two decades, resigned. Douglas had suffered a severe stroke in 1974. Although partly paralyzed and in great pain, Douglas continued to serve as a Justice for many months. When asked how he could cope with the work after he could no longer read, Douglas reportedly replied, "I'll listen and see how the Chief votes and vote the other way."[34]

Ironically, the choice of Douglas' replacement fell to President Gerald Ford, who had led an earlier congressional effort to impeach Douglas. Ford selected John Paul Stevens, another former corporate lawyer and a moderate Republican.[35] Stevens' arrival left the following line-up on the Bench.

---

31. 417 U.S. 600 (1974).

32. The *Griffin-Douglas* rule requires the government to provide certain free assistance for indigent criminal defendants. *See supra* pp. 144, 149.

33. Other illustrative decisions in the early 1970's adversely affecting the access of indigents to courts included *Edelman v. Jordan*, 415 U.S. 651 (1974) (initiating an eleventh amendment revolution by holding that the amendment bars an order requiring retroactive welfare payments); *Ortwein v. Schwab*, 410 U.S. 656 (1973) (upholding a filing fee for appeals from welfare rulings); and *United States v. Kras*, 409 U.S. 434 (1973) (upholding a filing fee for bankruptcy proceedings). *Cf. Milliken v. Bradley*, 418 U.S. 717 (1974) (banning desegregation orders against suburban school districts, absent proof that they participated in the segregation of inner-city schools).

34. Woodward & Armstrong, *The Brethren*, 391.

35. *See* R. Sickels, *John Paul Stevens and the Constitution* (1988); 5 Friedman & Israel, *The Justices of the United States*, 149–62. Ironically, the Douglas-Stevens succession may have nudged the Court to the left by eliminating the liberal wing's tendency to take extreme positions and by adding a strong, independent Justice to the Court's centrist bloc. In his first term, Stevens lined up a little left-of-center, closer to the Brennan-Marshall pole than to the Rehnquist-Burger pole. This slightly left-of-center alignment became standard for Stevens in most subsequent terms.

TABLE 24
Alignment of Justices, 1975

Left	Center	Right
Brennan	White	Rehnquist
Marshall	Stewart	Burger
	Stevens	Powell
		Blackmun

After Stevens' arrival, the Court continued its conservative retrenchment in many areas affecting the poor. The case which best illustrates the conservatism of the October 1974 Term is *Warth v. Seldin*,[36] the landmark standing case and *bete noir* of public interest lawyers. A variety of different individual and group plaintiffs challenged the exclusionary zoning law of Penfield, New York, a Rochester suburb, but failed to reach the merits of their equal protection claim after the Supreme Court held that all the claims must be dismissed on grounds such as standing, ripeness, and mootness. In *Warth*, the Nixon Court's door-closing strategy reached a new peak. As Douglas, Brennan, Marshall, and White pointed out in their dissent, the panoply of threshold barriers erected by the conservative majority made it nearly impossible for *anyone* to reach the merits of such a claim. But, of course, this was precisely the purpose of the four Nixonians.[37]

The poor suffered many losses during the mid-1970's. Welfare recipients lost a number of tough cases including some in which basic constitutional rights were clearly at stake.[38] Racial minorities suffered a series of defeats that seriously impaired the ability of federal courts to combat racial discrimination.[39] The Court also imposed new proce-

---

36. 422 U.S. 490 (1975).

37. The door-closing strategy was also evident in other cases decided in the October 1974 Term. *E.g., Hicks v. Miranda*, 422 U.S. 332 (1975) (extending the *Younger* nonintervention doctrine); *Jackson v. Metropolitan Edison Co.*, 419 U.S. 345 (1974) (narrowing both the public function and nexus strands of state action law).

38. *E.g., Trainor v. Hernandez*, 431 U.S. 434 (1977) (holding that federal courts may not enjoin an unconstitutional attachment of credit union funds owned by a person accused of welfare fraud); *Simon v. Eastern Kentucky Welfare Rights Org.*, 426 U.S. 26 (1976) (rejecting respondents' standing to sue).

39. *E.g., International Bhood. of Teamsters v. United States*, 431 U.S. 324 (1977) (signalling the end of liberal activism in employment discrimination cases); *Washington v. Davis*, 426 U.S. 229 (1976) (holding that the equal protection clause prohibits nonfacial racial discrimination only when accompanied by evil purpose to harm minorities); *Rizzo v. Goode*, 423 U.S. 362 (1976) (holding that claim of racial harassment by Philadelphia police does not present justiciable case).

dural barriers to public interest litigation.[40] In the antitrust field, the rule of thumb changed from "the government always wins" to "the government always loses."[41]

It was a conservative avalanche. A strong case can be made that the October 1975 Term was the most conservative term of the 1970's and that 1976, the nation's bicentennial, saw the fall of more economic and civil liberties than any year since the McCarthy era.

In general, the economic conservatism of the Nixon Court was carried out through procedural rulings, statutory interpretation, and constitutional restraint rather than activism. For the most part, the Bench did not return to the constitutional conservative activism that was the hallmark of its pre-1937 legacy. As the years passed, however, the Court majority did issue a few major decisions involving constitutional censorship of economic legislation. Five cases are especially noteworthy.

First, in *Edelman v. Jordan*,[42] the Court held that the eleventh amendment bars federal courts from ordering States to pay retroactive welfare benefits. This seminal case initiated a long line of decisions which built the eleventh amendment into a major barrier against federal court awards of money damages against States.[43]

The second and most famous was *National League of Cities v. Usery*,[44] which reactivated the tenth amendment as a limit on federal power to regulate the conduct of state and local governments. In this widely noted 5–4 decision, the Court struck down a federal minimum wage/maximum hour statute for public employees as a violation of state autonomy. In the process, the Court overruled a major Warren Court ruling that had gone the other way.[45]

---

40. *E.g., Piper v. Chris-Craft Indus. Inc.*, 430 U.S. 1 (1977) (narrowing implied private causes of action under federal statutes); *Alyeska v. Wilderness Soc'y*, 421 U.S. 240 (1975) (rejecting awards of attorneys' fees to successful litigants absent express statutory authorization); *Eisen v. Carlisle & Jacquelin*, 417 U.S. 156 (1974) (requiring plaintiffs to pay for notice to members of plaintiffs' class).

41. *E.g.*, Pollock, *Antitrust, the Supreme Court, the Spirit of '76*, 72 Northwestern U.L. Rev. 631 (1977).

42. 415 U.S. 651 (1974).

43. The liberal wing has dissented strongly in virtually all cases in this line right up to the time of this writing. All four members of the Rehnquist Court's moderate-liberal coalition agree that the majority's interpretation of the eleventh amendment is "egregiously wrong" and should be overturned.

44. 426 U.S. 833 (1976).

45. *Maryland v. Wirtz*, 392 U.S. 183 (1968). *National League of Cities* marks another milestone in the long line of fair labor standards cases that have provided so many

A third important case was *First National Bank v. Bellotti,*[46] which held that the first amendment prohibits States from restricting corporate expenditures designed to influence the outcome of referendum elections. Political speech is entitled to full first amendment protection, the five-vote majority held, regardless of whether its source is an individual or a business corporation. *Bellotti* was one in a string of cases restricting government power to control political speech by the rich and powerful.[47]

The remaining two cases resuscitated the contract clause as a potentially formidable barrier to economic reform legislation. In *United States Trust Co. v. New Jersey,*[48] a 4–3 majority held that New York and New Jersey could not repeal a covenant banning the use of bond revenues to subsidize rail transportation. This decision undercut the States' ability to respond to the 1970's energy crunch by shifting funds to mass transit facilities.

Finally, in *Allied Structural Steel Co. v. Spannaus,*[49] a five-vote majority held that the contract clause prohibited Minnesota from requiring employers who leave the State to pay assessments designed to insure pension benefits for former employees. Brennan's dissent bitterly criticized the decision, claiming that it threatened "to undermine the jurisprudence of property rights developed over the last 40 years."[50]

These five cases suggested that the Nixon Court of the mid-1970's was prepared to resume some constitutional censorship of economic legislation, even if the Justices were not ready to follow in the footsteps of the pre-1937 four horsemen and make conservative-activist war on the Great Society. All in all, the Nixon Court's 1972–77 heyday was a period of conservative retrenchment that seriously harmed the poor in their quest for economic justice.

C. The Conservative Trend Abates (1977–1982)

A trend toward moderation on the Supreme Court emerged in the

---

important examples in earlier chapters. These cases include *Lochner* (1905), *Muller* (1908), *Bunting* (1917), *Adkins* (1923), *Tipaldo* (1937), *Parrish* (1937), and *Wirtz* (1968).

46. 435 U.S. 765 (1978).

47. *E.g., Buckley v. Valeo,* 424 U.S. 1 (1976).

48. 431 U.S. 1 (1977).

49. 438 U.S. 234 (1978). This case is a little out of the relevant time period; it is mentioned here because of its obvious connection to *United States Trust Co.*

50. *Id.,* 259.

late 1970's, coinciding with a more moderate pattern in American politics.[51] From 1977 to 1981, the middle-of-the-road Democrat Jimmy Carter occupied the White House, and liberals had a stronger hand in Congress. The abatement of the conservative trend that marked the Nixon and Ford years was a minor one, not enough to produce a separate period of either American or Supreme Court history, but it provided a change of pace from the conservative dominance that preceded and followed it.

The softening of conservative dominance on the Burger Court had several causes. The Supreme Court pendulum often moves back toward the center after a swing to the right or left extreme. Moreover, the mid-1970's saw some alignment shifts on the Court. As mentioned above, Stevens' arrival in 1975 gave additional credibility to the Court's moderate, centrist group. At the same time, White loosened his ties with the four Nixonians. Most important, however, Harry Blackmun shifted dramatically to the left. The four Nixonians became a trio, and they now faced the more difficult task of obtaining two votes from a six-vote pool of moderates and liberals. By the end of the October 1976 Term, "The center was in control."[52]

The October 1977 Term was the first in which these new patterns became clear. Voting profiles for that term were strikingly different from prior terms. White was statistically left of the Court's center for the first time since the October 1963 Term. Stewart moved to the left into a position almost exactly in the center between the Rehnquist-Burger and Brennan-Marshall poles. Blackmun moved sharply to the left, disagreeing with Rehnquist nearly as frequently as with Brennan and Marshall. Even Powell broke from Rehnquist and Burger and moved into a position near the Court's center. As a result, the Court had a 2–5–2 alignment in the October 1977 Term. Rehnquist and Burger promptly posted dissent rates up a third from the prior term, while Brennan and Marshall posted lower dissent rates that were about the same as Rehnquist and Burger's.

The shift to the left during the October 1977 Term was reflected in a series of liberal victories, some of which involved economic issues. *Memphis Light, Gas & Water Division v. Craft,*[53] for example, held that procedural due process guarantees customers at least an informal

---

51. *See* Galloway, *The Burger Court (1969–1986)*, 27 Santa Clara L. Rev. 31, 44–52 (1987).
52. Woodward & Armstrong, *The Brethren*, 444.
53. 436 U.S. 1 (1978).

chance to be heard prior to termination of gas and electricity.[54] *Monell v. Department of Social Services*[55] overruled a William O. Douglas decision and held that municipal corporations are subject to suit under 42 U.S.C. 1983 when they violate constitutional or statutory rights.[56] *Monell* was a seminal case that generated a long line of progeny and opened up an important field of civil liberties litigation against local government agencies. And, in one of the most famous cases of the decade, *Board of Regents v. Bakke*,[57] the Court held that race-conscious affirmative action programs do not *per se* violate the equal protection clause.[58]

The leftward trend in the October 1977 Term, however, was far from a liberal sweep. Rehnquist and Burger retained a slight edge over Brennan and Marshall in the won-lost column, and the conservatives won some major victories. *Bakke*, for example, held that the special admissions program at University of California, Davis Medical School violated the equal protection clause because it unnecessarily used a quota.[59] Similarly, *Allied Structural Steel Co. v. Spannaus*[60] revived the contract clause as a barrier to economic reform legislation.[61] Both *Bakke* and *Spannaus* were landmark cases demonstrating that the Burger Court was still capable of imposing constitutional barriers to economic reform efforts.

Over the next few years, the Court oscillated between the conservative dominance that had prevailed in the mid-1970's and the more moderate pattern that emerged in 1977. Powell moved quickly back into close alignment with Burger, but Blackmun did not. Table 25 shows the line-up that emerged in the late 1970's and lasted for the most part until Stewart's 1981 resignation.

---

54. Rehnquist, Burger, and Stevens dissented.
55. 436 U.S. 658 (1978).
56. Rehnquist and Burger dissented.
57. 438 U.S. 265 (1978).
58. Rehnquist, Burger, Stewart, and Stevens dissented.
59. Brennan, Marshall, Blackmun, and White dissented from this aspect of *Bakke*.
60. 436 U.S. 234 (1978).
61. *See supra* p. 162.

TABLE 25
Alignment of Justices, 1978–80

Left	Center	Right
Brennan	Stewart	Rehnquist
Marshall	White	Burger
	Blackmun	Powell
	Stevens	

The most important benefits for the poor resulting from the Burger Court's more moderate "middle period" concerned the rights of economic underdogs such as racial minorities. Most important was *United Steelworkers v. Weber*,[62] the landmark affirmative action case upholding a racial quota requiring that 50% of the participants in a craft training program be black. *Weber* revived the affirmative action movement by holding that Title VII of the Civil Rights Act of 1964 does not prohibit temporary remedial racial discrimination designed to correct racial imbalances in traditionally segregated job classifications.[63] *Weber* was followed by *Fullilove v. Klutznick*,[64] which upheld a federal statute requiring that 10% of all contract dollars on federally funded public works construction projects be set aside for minority business enterprises.

The Court's more moderate posture in the civil rights field was underscored by the remarkable decision in *Dayton Board of Education v. Brinkman*,[65] which repaired some of the damage to school desegregation litigation inflicted by the conservative onslaught in the mid-1970's. The main problem was the *Davis-Feeney* "evil purpose" test adopted by the Nixon Court to eliminate equal protection challenges to non-facial racial classifications. Apparently realizing that plaintiffs in school desegregation cases would normally not be able to satisfy the stringent evil purpose test, the Court adopted an "adverse impact" test for this single area of law, holding that plaintiffs who prove *de jure* segregation in the past may prevail by showing recent decisions by defendants having the *effect* of perpetuating or exacerbating the separation of public school students. The narrow 5–4 victory for the moderate-liberal coalition was made possible by the swing votes of White and Blackmun.[66]

---

62. 443 U.S. 193 (1979).
63. Rehnquist and Burger dissented.
64. 448 U.S. 448 (1980).
65. 443 U.S. 526 (1979).
66. Rehnquist, Burger, Powell, and Stewart dissented. Rehnquist pointed out, cor-

Of course, the more moderate trend that emerged in the late 1970's was punctuated by many conservative victories. In *Scott v. Illinois*,[67] for example, the Court cut back on *Gideon v. Wainwright*,[68] one of the Warren Court's most famous landmarks, by holding that indigent criminal defendants do not have a sixth amendment right to assistance of counsel in prosecutions that do not result in actual imprisonment. Similarly, in *Lassiter v. Department of Social Services*,[69] the Court held that indigent parents do not have a constitutional right to court-appointed counsel in proceedings to terminate parental rights.[70]

In 1980, a presidential election occurred that would prove critical to the balance of power on the Supreme Court. In that year, Ronald Reagan, a right-wing Republican previously thought so extreme as to be unelectable, was chosen by a nation tired of runaway inflation and international humiliation. Reagan promptly initiated the most far-reaching effort since Franklin D. Roosevelt to pack the federal courts with judges chosen on the basis of their political and economic ideology. The Court-packing project was directed by Reagan's advisor Edwin Meese III, who set up a procedure for insuring that nominees for the federal bench pass an ideological litmus test designed to screen out all but true believers in the Reagan Revolution.

In 1981, a change in Supreme Court personnel brought the first Reagan appointee and first woman Justice to the Bench and set the stage for a return to conservative dominance. Potter Stewart, a moderate conservative, resigned at the end of the October 1980 Term. Reagan offered the seat to White House counsellor Meese, but Meese declined. The Reagan-Meese team then nominated Sandra Day O'Connor, a "Goldwater Republican" from Arizona and former Stanford Law School classmate of Justice Rehnquist.[71] O'Connor's voting record after arriving on the Court was so conservative that TIME Magazine dubbed Rehnquist and O'Connor the "Arizona Twins."[72]

The Stewart-O'Connor succession was an important one. Blackmun's defection in 1977 had made it more difficult for the conservative

---

rectly, that the Court's adverse impact test was unprecedented under the equal protection clause and was based on a "cascade of presumptions" contrary to normal evidentiary inferences.

67. 440 U.S. 367 (1979).

68. 372 U.S. 335 (1963). *See supra p. 145.*

69. 452 U.S. 18 (1981).

70. Brennan and Marshall dissented in both cases.

71. For a detailed account of O'Connor's career, see E. Witt, *A Different Justice* (1986).

72. *And Now, The Arizona Twins,* TIME, April 19, 1982, at 49.

wing to dominate the Court. Goldwater Republican O'Connor was a perfect candidate to fill the gap in the right wing. The "four horsepersons," Rehnquist, Burger, O'Connor, and Powell, replaced the four Nixonians as the strongest bloc on the Court,[73] and it appeared in October 1981 that a new era of conservative dominance had begun.

Surprisingly, however, the conservatives did *not* dominate the October 1981 Term. Instead, the moderate trend that began in 1977 continued. Dissent rates dropped substantially on the left and rose substantially on the right. For the first time since the October 1969 Term, dissent rates were higher on the right than on the left. Indeed, Rehnquist posted the highest dissent rate on the 1981–82 Court.

Demonstrating the Court's continuing, less conservative mood, the liberals broke new ground in *Plyler v. Doe*,[74] holding that requiring children of undocumented workers to pay public school tuition violates the equal protection clause. The case was a landmark because the five-vote majority invoked intensified scrutiny even though, technically, the classification was not suspect and the right was not fundamental. Somewhat suspect classifications burdening somewhat fundamental rights are subject to an intermediate presumption of unconstitutionality, the Court held, opening up a new line of equal protection law.[75]

In summary, after trailing badly in the mid-1970's, the Supreme Court's liberal wing staged something of a comeback in late 1970's and early 1980's, ushering in a somewhat more moderate interlude in the predominantly conservative Burger era.[76] As the statistical balance of power shifted to the left, the Court seemed to pause, to consolidate the many changes made in the heyday of the Nixon Court, and to curtail a few of the harsh results caused by the earlier conservative onslaught.

---

73. The nickname "four horsepersons" derives from the four horsemen nickname used in the 1930's to describe the conservative activists Van Devanter, McReynolds, Sutherland, and Butler. With a woman on board, "four horsemen—part II" is obviously out.

74. 457 U.S. 745 (1982).

75. Rehnquist, Burger, O'Connor, and White dissented. Powell was the Justice who broke away from the conservative bloc and gave the victory to the moderate-liberal coalition. Powell's role as "man in the middle" was to become a major theme of Supreme Court history for the rest of his tenure. The 1987–88 Powell-Kennedy succession suggests that *Plyler* may be a derelict on the waters of the law.

76. This moderate interlude may profitably be compared to the not quite progressive interlude in the Court's second conservative era, the conservative Vinson Court interlude in the Court's second liberal era, and the restrained, conservative interlude in the Warren era.

D. Conservative Dominance (1982–1986)

The Burger Court made its expected return to the right in the October 1982 Term. Once again, the conservatives began winning most of the close splits and prevailing in the won-lost column by a substantial margin. O'Connor lent strong support to the resurgent right wing, posting the second most conservative voting record on the Court and ousting Burger from his accustomed spot next to Rehnquist.

Powerful evidence of renewed conservative dominance appeared during the June 1983 crunch. Marshall dissented in 18 of the last 22 cases. Brennan joined him in 16. Blackmun, who was far to the left of the Court's statistical center that term, dissented in 12. Stevens dissented in 9.[77]

The renewed conservative dominance was even more striking in the October 1983 Term. Throughout 1984, the conservatives posted one major victory after another, leading Court watchers to the consensus that the Burger-Rehnquist bloc had at last achieved the control over the Court that Nixon, Reagan, Meese, and other conservatives had so long awaited.[78]

NLRB v. Bildisco[79] epitomizes the conservative trend. This was a period of union busting, triggered by President Reagan's firing of thousands of striking air traffic controllers in 1981. Encouraged by the President and the increasingly conservative Court, corporate managers tried a new way to weaken unions, bankruptcy. In *Bildisco*, the Court held that companies may unilaterally suspend collective bargaining agreements by filing bankruptcy. Brennan, Marshall, Blackmun, and White dissented.

---

77. The most important of these decisions involved civil liberties rather than economics. *E.g., Michigan v. Long*, 463 U.S. 1032 (1983) (fourth amendment); *Mueller v. Allen*, 463 U.S. 388 (1983) (establishment clause).

78. *E.g.,* Kilpatrick, *Supreme Court's Term Had Conservative Tone*, Casper Star-Tribune, July 12, 1984, at A10, cols. 1–2. As Kilpatrick put it,

> For the better part of 15 years, since Warren Earl Burger became chief justice, American conservatives have been praying for the day when the Supreme Court would turn decisively from the judicial liberalism that characterized the court of Earl Warren. In the term that ended July 5, their prayers were answered at last.... [T]he Court's four relatively consistent conservatives—Burger, Rehnquist, O'Connor and Powell—finally got their act together. They formed a solid working coalition with Justice White and occasionally with Justice Blackmun. The result was nearly total frustration for the liberal wing.

79. 465 U.S. 513 (1984).

The same term, the Court sent strong signals that the more moderate era in civil rights had ended. In *Grove City College v. Bell*,[80] the Court gutted Title IX of the Education Amendments of 1972 by holding that the statutory ban on discrimination by federally funded entities extends only to the specific division receiving the funds. Thus, Grove City College, a recipient of federal student loans, could discriminate as long as the office administering the loans complied with federal nondiscrimination requirements.[81] *Firefighters Local Union No. 1748 v. Stotts*[82] raised serious doubts about the future of affirmative action by suggesting in *dicta* that remedial racial preferences must be limited to "identified victims of past discrimination."[83]

After the conservative onslaught in early 1984, many commentators speculated that the Court had entered a reactionary period and that Rehnquist, Burger, O'Connor, Powell, and White were leading the Court in what Harry Blackmun called a "rightward plunge." Here is how the Washington Post's Court correspondents described the situation at the start of the October 1984 Term.

> A string of conservative victories in decisions last year and the expectations of similar gains this term have caused unprecedented anxiety in liberal quarters. . . . Some liberals, like Burt Neuborne, legal director of the American Civil Liberties Union, say they wish the curtain would never come up on the Supreme Court term that is about to begin. "I feel like the general Napoleon left behind to cover his retreat from Russia," Neuborne said. . . . Even Vincent Blasi, the Columbia University Law Professor who last year published a book called "The Burger Court: The Counter-Revolution that Wasn't," says that after last term, all bets are off on that title. "The premises have changed," Blasi said. "We may be in a new era."[84]

---

80. 465 U.S. 555 (1984).

81. The *Grove City College* decision generated a storm of criticism by civil rights leaders and ultimately was overturned by federal statute.

82. 467 U.S. 561 (1984). Brennan, Marshall, and Blackmun dissented.

83. In the first half of 1984, the conservative wing also won a series of landmark victories in cases not directly involving rich-poor issues. *E.g., United States v. Leon*, 468 U.S. 897 (1984) (adopting reasonableness exception to the fourth amendment exclusionary rule); *Regan v. Wald*, 468 U.S. 222 (1984) (upholding restrictions on travel to Cuba); *Schall v. Martin*, 467 U.S. 253 (1984) (upholding preventive detention of juveniles); *Lynch v. Donnelly*, 466 U.S. 994 (1984) (upholding government nativity scene against establishment clause challenge).

84. Berbash & Kamen, *Supreme Court To Address Church-State Relations, Police Powers*, Washington Post, Sept. 30, 1984, at A4, col. 1.

But the Court has a way of surprising commentators by turning back toward the center after a plunge to either extreme. As the 1984–85 term unfolded, the liberal wing fared unexpectedly well. In the words of Congressional Quarterly's Elder Witt, "[T]he Court moved back toward the moderate center and away from the unremitting conservatism of the previous Term."[85] By early 1985, articles began to appear claiming a "dramatic reversal" in the Court's previously reactionary pattern.[86]

The reversal produced striking results in the economic arena. The biggest landmark of the term was *Garcia v. San Antonio Metropolitan Transit Authority*,[87] which overruled *National League of Cities v. Usery*[88] and put the tenth amendment back into retirement. *Garcia* held that the federal government may impose minimum wage and overtime requirements on local government agencies. As in *Usery*, the split was 5–4; Blackmun changed sides, joining the four *Usery* dissenters and writing the majority opinion holding that the tenth amendment does not impose judicially enforceable limits on Congress.[89]

The conservative wing came on with a rush, however, in the 1985 end-of-term crunch and salvaged their statistical dominance. Moreover, the conservative bloc dominated the October 1985 Term, the final term of the Burger Court, as well. That term Marshall and Brennan cast more dissents than all five conservatives.

Table 26 shows the line-up during the October 1985 Term and, more generally, during most of the 1982–86 period.

---

85. Witt, *A Different Justice*, 2.

86. *E.g.*, Kamen, *High Court Reverses Trend: Individuals Win More Civil Liberties Cases*, Washington Post, May 5, 1985, at A1, col. 2. An illustrative civil-liberties victory was *Wallace v. Jaffree*, 472 U.S. 38 (1985) (school prayer).

87. 469 U.S. 528 (1985).

88. 426 U.S. 833 (1976). *See supra* p. 161.

89. Indigents also won an important victory during the term in *Ake v. Oklahoma*, 470 U.S. 68 (1985), which held that an indigent criminal defendant was entitled to a court-appointed psychiatrist to assist in an insanity defense.

TABLE 26
Alignment of Justices, 1982–86

Left	Center	Right
Brennan	Stevens	Rehnquist
Marshall	Blackmun	Burger
		O'Connor
		Powell
		White

The dominance of the four horsepersons was secured by White's surprisingly strong support. Indeed, White was statistically third from the right in the 1984–85 term. In contrast, Blackmun ended the Burger Era third from the left, posting much higher disagreement rates with Rehnquist (45.1%) and his erstwhile Minnesota Twin Burger (37.0%) than with Marshall (20.1%) and Brennan (21.4%).

To summarize, the Burger era (1969–86) was, in general, a period of conservative dominance on the United States Supreme Court. From 1969 to 1972, the Court swung sharply away from the liberal activism characteristic of the late Warren Court. By January 1972, the four Nixonians—Burger, Blackmun, Powell, and Rehnquist—had been seated, and they dominated the 1972–77 Court, carrying out a far-reaching counterattack on Warren-brand liberal activism. Stevens' 1975 arrival and Harry Blackmun's 1977 shift out of the conservative bloc caused control to pass to the Court's "floating center" from 1977 to 1982. However, O'Connor's 1981 arrival and White's swing to the right restored the prevailing pattern of conservative dominance on the 1982–86 Court.

The Burger Court's conservatism was reflected in a long series of decisions which strengthened the hand of the police, weakened the enforcement of civil rights and civil liberties, increased the legal immunities of State governments, and hastened the retreat from federal programs designed to achieve distributive economic justice. Overall, the Burger Court was more like the restrained, conservative 1949–53 Vinson Court than the liberal-activist 1937–46 Roosevelt Court and 1962–69 Warren Court.

16

The Rehnquist Court (1986–1990)

The Rehnquist era began on October 6, 1986, when William Hubbs Rehnquist was sworn in as Chief Justice of the United States. Rehnquist, the most conservative Associate Justice since McReynolds, had posted the most conservative voting statistics *every* term since 1972. The same day, the conservative wing was strengthened by the arrival of another conservative, Antonin Scalia, Reagan's nominee for the Associate Justiceship left open by Rehnquist's promotion. The Rehnquist-Scalia appointments were a double-barrelled blast by Reagan and Meese against the Warren-brand liberal activism Meese so detested.

Rehnquist's promotion kept the crucial Chief Justiceship in the Court's far-right bloc. Although just one vote out of nine, the Chief has important powers that can be used to control the direction of Supreme Court law. The Chief assigns the majority opinion whenever he is in the majority. He gives the opening statement in every case that comes before the Conference for discussion and decision. He presides at oral arguments and administers the federal judiciary.

To fill the seat left open by Rehnquist's promotion, Reagan and Meese narrowed the field to two candidates, Antonin Scalia and Robert Bork, the two leaders of the D.C. Circuit's rejuvenated conservative wing. Ultimately Scalia was selected because he was as gifted and conservative as Bork and twenty years younger. A conservative from his youth, Scalia was described by his former partner David Snow as "one of the first Bill Buckley-type conservatives."[1] Daniel Elliot, another former partner, says, "I recall the guy vividly. He was a real hard core Goldwater person."[2] Scalia's arrival strengthened the conservative wing, because he was younger, more energetic, smarter, and even more conservative than Burger.

The line-up during the first term of the Rehnquist era was four conservatives, three centrists, and two liberals. As usual, Rehnquist was on the far right, disagreeing with both Marshall and Brennan in 61.8% of

---

1. S. Adler, *Live Wire on the D.C. Circuit*, LEGAL TIMES, June 23, 1986, at 10, col. 4.
2. *Id.*

the cases. As expected, Scalia moved into Burger's old second-from-the-right slot, disagreeing with both Marshall and Brennan in 53.9% of the cases. Next came White and O'Connor. They too disagreed with Marshall and Brennan in over half the cases. In his final term, Powell was, as the papers said, the "man in the middle,"[3] but he remained well right of the. Court's statistical center. Stevens and Blackmun were somewhat left of center statistically. Brennan and Marshall were, as usual, alone on the far left.

The Rehnquist Court's first term began less conservatively than expected. The liberals won the term's first five major cases and Scalia raised some eyebrows by joining the liberals in two of the five.[4] The most important liberal victory was *Johnson v. Transportation Agency*,[5] which held that promoting a woman rather than a marginally more qualified man to fill a position in a previously segregated job did not violate Title VII of the Civil Rights Act of 1964.[6]

Soon, however, Scalia moved into close alignment with Rehnquist, and the conservative wing took control. By the end of the term, Marshall, Brennan, Blackmun, and Stevens had cast nearly 60% of the dissents. The liberals were buried by a blizzard of conservative decisions.

In the economic arena, the term's blockbuster cases involved the takings clause. *First English Evangelical Lutheran Church v. County of Los Angeles*[7] resolved one of the most notoriously "open" constitutional questions of the day by holding that compensation must be awarded for temporary regulatory takings. *Nollan v. California Coastal Commission*[8] held that requiring a property owner to grant public access to the beach as a condition for obtaining a building permit comprises a regulatory taking for which compensation must be paid. These landmark cases suggested that the dominant Rehnquist-Scalia bloc was ready to engage in some conservative constitutional activism of the pre-1937 type.

The same term, the conservative wing expanded governmental immunities from personal injury claims by holding that the victims of the

---

3. Repa, *Powell Was the High Court's Man in the Middle*, San Francisco Chronicle, June 27, 1987, at 9, col. 1.

4. *INS v. Cardoza-Fonseca*, 107 S. Ct. 1207 (1987) (asylum); *California Federal S.&L. Ass'n v. Guerra*, 107 S. Ct. 683 (1987) (pregnancy leave).

5. 107 S. Ct. 1942 (1987).

6. Rehnquist, Scalia, and White dissented.

7. 107 S. Ct. 2378 (1987).

8. 107 S. Ct. 3141 (1987).

Army's infamous LSD experiments may not sue the government for damages.[9]

Justice Powell prevented conservative dominance from turning into a conservative rout during the first term of the Rehnquist era. As mentioned above, Powell had been viewed as the "man in the middle" ever since O'Connor arrived and White turned to the right. In the 1986–87 term he was, in fact, the Justice closest to the Court's statistical center. Powell's vote was especially critical to the moderate-liberal coalition in "social agenda" cases involving abortion, affirmative action, and separation of church and state. Therefore, when Powell retired at the end of the term in June 1987, the stage was set for a major confrontation.

President Reagan and Attorney General Meese rose to the bait. For years they had hoped to use the Court to implement the social agenda they could never get through Congress. Knowing the golden opportunity was at hand, Reagan and Meese nominated Robert Bork, a brilliant legal scholar and arch-conservative D.C. Circuit Judge. That set off the epochal 1987 Battle for the Court.[10]

Throughout the summer and fall of 1987 the battle over the Bork nomination raged. The nomination catalyzed the liberal coalition like nothing in years. A Court dominated by Bork, Rehnquist, Scalia, O'-Connor, and White would have posed grave dangers to civil rights, the right of privacy (including abortion), free speech, the fourth amendment, workers' rights, and much, much more. Many of these issues were discussed in detail during the televised Senate Judiciary Committee hearings. Bork's testimony, including his celebrated debate with Pennsylvania's Republican Senator Arlen Specter, electrified the nation in a way that no Supreme Court event had done in years. In the end, a national consensus against turning back the clock on civil rights and putting the government into the bedroom doomed the nomination. On Oct. 23, 1987, the Senate rejected Bork by a 58–42 vote.

With the Bork battle still raging and Powell's successor not yet confirmed, the Supreme Court opened its October 1987 Term. A four-vote conservative bloc confronted a four-vote moderate-liberal coalition. The Court was deadlocked. As a result, the Court was on hold during much of the term. For months, the Justices dodged the major cases, dismissing one potential landmark case for want of jurisdiction, sending another back to State court for further instructions on State law, and dividing evenly on two more. Although a few landmark decisions were

9. *United States v. Stanley*, 107 S. Ct. 3054 (1987).
10. E. Bronner, *Battle for Justice* (1989).

handed down, the period from October 1987 until the seating of Powell's successor was a backwater of Supreme Court history. Perhaps the most interesting development was that O'Connor, after several terms of more moderate voting, posted the most conservative voting record of the term, ousting Rehnquist from the far right position he had held since 1972.

After Bork's nomination went down in flames and the nomination of Douglas Ginzburg went up in smoke,[11] Reagan nominated Ninth Circuit Judge Anthony Kennedy for the vacant seat. Widely viewed as the most moderate nominee that could be expected from the Reagan-Meese team, Kennedy was easily confirmed by a Senate suffering from "institutional exhaustion" after the Bork battle. Kennedy was considered a centrist on the Ninth Circuit, and the big question after his seating in February 1988 was whether he would move into Powell's slot as man in the middle or come down farther to the right in the vicinity of Rehnquist and Scalia.[12]

Kennedy's arrival marked the start of the fully mature Reagan Court. At that point, four Justices owed their current seats to Reagan. "Meese's pieces"—Rehnquist, Scalia, and O'Connor—were products of the Meese litmus test. Kennedy, although not a Meese selection, was an old Sacramento friend of then California Governor Reagan and his advisor Meese. If Kennedy joined the conservative wing and White continued his swing to the right, conservative dominance would continue.

The other shoe fell during the October 1988 Term. To the surprise of many, Justice Kennedy staked out a position deep in the conservative wing, second from the right, near Rehnquist and Scalia.[13] With Kennedy moving almost lock-step with Rehnquist, and White providing

---

11. Ginzburg, a judge on the D.C. Circuit, was Meese's second choice for Powell's seat. Ginzburg had described himself as the most conservative lawyer in the Meese Justice Department, which included Meese himself and his conservative assistant William Bradford Reynolds. Ginzburg asked that his name be withdrawn after the news broke that he had smoked marijuana when he was a law professor at Harvard.

12. Kennedy participated in 71 cases during his first term; his voting pattern was moderately conservative.

13. "Conservatives got more of what they were looking for ideologically than they would have gotten with Bob Bork," said conservative Court watcher Gary McDowell. Kamen, *Why the Court Turned Right,* San Francisco Chronicle, April 12, 1989, at A9, cols. 2–3. "Anthony Kennedy's performance on the Supreme Court is what all those raving lunatics who opposed Bob Bork deserve," added Daniel Popeo, another conservative commentator. *Id.,* col. 2.

the fifth vote, the Court issued a series of conservative decisions that stunned liberals.[14] When the dust settled and the votes were counted, it was clear that a new conservative bloc, the five horsepersons—Rehnquist, Scalia, Kennedy, O'Connor, and White—had taken over the Court and initiated an even more conservative and activist chapter in the Supreme Court's third conservative era.

The biggest Court story of the term was the Missouri abortion case, *Webster v. Reproductive Health Services*,[15] which upheld a Missouri statute imposing a series of restrictions on the right of abortion, including a requirement that post-20-week abortions be preceded by a fetal viability test. Without explicitly overruling *Roe v. Wade*,[16] the Court cut back dramatically on constitutional protections for abortions, restored substantial power to state legislatures to restrict abortions, and set the stage for 1989's most intense political battles. The Missouri abortion case primarily jeopardized the poor, since rich pregnant women have no problem getting abortions.

By far the most important development in the economic arena, however, was a series of landmark cases turning the clock back on civil rights. The first and perhaps the most important decision was *City of Richmond v. J.A. Croson Co.*,[17] which struck down Richmond, Virginia's affirmative action program requiring that 30% of public works construction dollars be set aside for minority business enterprises. *Croson* stood the equal protection clause on its head, converting it from a bulwark of equality to a guarantee of inequality and holding, for the first time ever, that governmental affirmative action programs containing remedial racial classifications are unconstitutional unless strict scrutiny is satisfied.

In June 1989, the Court handed minorities and women one civil rights defeat after another. *Wards Cove Packing Co. v. Atonio*[18] gutted Title VII of the Civil Rights Act of 1964 by shifting the burden of persuasion on the crucial issue of business necessity from employers to em-

---

14. Dissent rates within the moderate-liberal coalition skyrocketed. Marshall's dissent rate jumped by nearly two-thirds to 41.2%, a personal record and one of the highest dissent rates in the Court's history. The dissent rates of Brennan, Blackmun, and Stevens jumped by more than 50%, and both Brennan and Blackmun set new personal records. The four members of the moderate-liberal coalition cast 182 dissents, while the five conservatives cast only 81.

15. 109 S. Ct. 3040 (1989).

16. 410 U.S. 113 (1973).

17. 109 S. Ct. 706 (1989).

18. 109 S. Ct. 2115 (1989).

ployees. Calling the decision "close to the death knell" for disparate impact cases, E. Richard Larson, author of a leading treatise on employment discrimination law said, "It's devastating, a total change of the law."[19] *Patterson v. McLean Credit Union*[20] gutted the Civil Rights Act of 1866, holding that it does not create a cause of action for racial harassment during the employment relationship. And the Court issued four other decisions inflicting major defeats on minorities and women. The New York Times commented, "Today's Supreme Court majority sides with the beneficiaries, not the victims, of discrimination."[21]

At the time of this writing, it appears that a new and even more conservative period in the Court's third conservative era began in 1988. The five horsepersons—Rehnquist, Scalia, Kennedy, O'Connor, and White—dominated the 1988–90 Court and are prepared to implement the Nixon-Reagan agenda in an activist fashion. Marshall and Brennan—the paleo-liberals—were isolated on the left and dissenting more than ever before in the 1988–89 and 1989–90 terms. Blackmun and Stevens—the bleeding-heart moderates—remained somewhat left of center and were also dissenting at or near record levels for them.[22] On the Court's two hundredth birthday, the line-up was as follows.

TABLE 27
Alignment of Justices, 1990

Left	Center	Right
Brennan	Stevens	Rehnquist
Marshall	Blackmun	Scalia
		Kennedy
		White
		O'Connor

In the summer of 1990, William J. Brennan retired. A champion of the poor and weak, Brennan had been the playmaker of the moderate-liberal coalition. To replace Brennan, President George Bush chose David H. Souter, a conservative New Hampshire judge. Souter's alignment on the future Court is unknown, but it seems likely that he will join the Rehnquist bloc, giving the conservatives a solid six-vote majority.

19. San Francisco Chronicle, June 6, 1989, at A20, col. 1.
20. 109 S. Ct. 2363 (1989).
21. New York Times, June 14, 1989, at A18, col. 2.
22. The nickname "bleeding-heart moderates" derives from Blackmun's speech several years ago claiming "the center held, but it bled."

Moreover, the Court may become more conservative in the next few years. The two oldest Justices are Marshall (82) and Blackmun (82), the Court's two most liberal members. If either dies or retires, President Bush will have the chance to push the Court still further to the right. If Marshall departs, the nation will have a Court without liberals.

For the moment, the Powell-Kennedy and Brennan-Souter successions have pushed the already conservative Rehnquist Court still further to the right and made the prospects for the poor at the bar of the Supreme Court poor indeed.

17
Conclusions

The first major conclusion suggested by this study is that the United States Supreme Court is and always has been a political body which often decides cases on the basis of socio-economic values rather than value-neutral legal rules. This fact has been recognized by legal scholars and practitioners for years, but it tends to be overlaid by the myth that judges are merely technicians who discover and apply the law in an objective manner. The data from Supreme Court history suggest that the myth is entirely untrue.

From the start, Presidents have selected Justices primarily because of their economic and political views. This has been true for Washington, Jefferson, Lincoln, Taft, Wilson, Franklin Roosevelt, Nixon, Reagan, and many others. Moreover, once on the Court, Justices have tended to vote repeatedly in tightly-knit blocs on the main economic issues, so that Supreme Court adjudication becomes largely a matter of political head-counting similar to the decision-making process in the House and Senate, rather than a quest for the single correct and just answer to legal problems.

Indeed, a characteristic of most issues regarding the distribution of wealth is that fully rational philosophies exist to justify both the conservative and liberal viewpoints. Thus, in close cases, the decision will depend primarily on the Justices' preferences and will not be controlled by objective inquiry into legal principles.

However, although Justices are political animals selected largely on the basis of their political and economic beliefs, Presidents have frequently been disappointed in the judicial performance of their appointees. The future behavior of Supreme Court Justices has proved to be somewhat unpredictable. James Madison's selection of the conservative Story was the first major presidential mistake of this nature. Theodore Roosevelt's frustration at Holmes' refusal to enforce antitrust laws vigorously is notorious. Wilson's error in nominating McReynolds was fatal to the prospects for a truly progressive Court in the World War I era. And Eisenhower's disgust at Warren's liberal activism is well known.

Nevertheless, despite these exceptions, Presidents have usually done rather well in selecting Justices whose views on major issues matched their own. Washington, Jackson, Harding, Franklin Roosevelt, and Nixon, for example, succeeded in creating new Courts—indeed new eras of Supreme Court history—that reflected their political and economic views.

Another conclusion suggested by the historical materials covered in this book is that none of the common images regarding the role of the Supreme Court is adequate to cover the Court's entire history. The Court changes. It is a shapeshifter which, at times, has resembled each of three different profiles. It has been a servant of the rich, a champion of the poor, *and* a neutral mediator among interest groups.

During the first conservative era (1790–1835), the Court functioned— albeit often in a rather restrained way—as a protector of the wealthy. Under the leadership of Marshall and Story, the Court was committed to the twin pillars of the Federalists, nationalism and economic conservatism.

During the first liberal era (1836–1890), the Court assumed a role somewhat like that of a neutral mediator between the rich and the poor. Throughout much of this second period, the Court was perhaps more sympathetic with the needs of the poor. Nevertheless, the Court's personnel were recruited mainly from the class of corporate lawyers, so there was no shortage of empathy with the desires of expanding capitalism. Moreover, the Court certainly did not view itself as the "champion" of the poor or as the initiator of economic reform programs.

During the second conservative era (1890–1937), the Court assumed a role very close to that ascribed to it by its more aggressive left-wing critics, namely, handmaiden to the corporate rich. Starting in the 1890's, the Court undertook a campaign to prevent the people of the United States from making structural changes necessary to bridge the gap from the frontier abundance of early America to the urban-industrial America of the twentieth century. This campaign was waged on behalf of the rich and was designed to prevent the people from regulating private wealth.

During the period after 1937, the Court largely returned to the role of mediator between conflicting interests. For a brief period in the 1960's, the Court began to resemble the third image and to function as champion of the poor. This phase in the Court's history was cut short by the judicial appointments and political trends of the Nixon period.

The longest portion of the Court's history (including the 114 years from 1790 to 1835, 1890 to 1937, and 1969 to 1990) has been characterized by a definite partiality for the rich. To a large extent, this was the result of policies held by the founding fathers and written into the Constitution. It seems uncontestable that the drafters of the Constitution intended to place the rights of private property in a preferred position and to assign to the Supreme Court the duty of guarding that position. In other words, there was an original *explicit* intention that the Court function as special protector of the wealthy. Thus, in order to transcend this role, the Court had to break away from the instructions contained in its own charter and redefine its purpose to fit changing social needs.

Even after the Court succeeded in breaking out of its original role as protector of the wealthy, it did not, for the most part, function as champion of the poor. Of the three common images, this one is by far the least descriptive of the Court's actual behavior. Only during a relatively few years in the 1940's, 1950's, and 1960's did the Court become an advocate and initiator of economic reform, and the Burger and Rehnquist Courts have left no doubt that they consider the experiment to be at an end. In short, the Supreme Court has usually alternated between roles as protector of the rich and as neutral mediator and has only rarely assumed the role of champion of the poor.

Another conclusion suggested by the historical materials is that the Court, for all its theoretical independence, is quite responsive to pressure from public opinion and from the political branches. From Marshall's suggestion that Congress be given power to reverse the Court's constitutional rulings to the Court's astonishing 1937 revolution in the face of FDR's Court-packing proposal and beyond, the Court has normally retreated when subjected to sustained majority opposition. Without the power of the purse or the sword, the Court is sustained only by public acceptance and therefore must normally stay within limits set by public opinion.

The Court has been able, on the one hand, to write the views of its controlling majority into law and, on the other hand, to stage orderly retreats in the face of strong public pressure largely because of the extraordinary flexibility of its doctrinal tools. In most cases, the Court has the sovereign prerogative of choice, as Cardozo put it. The Court is free to discard old rules and invent new ones when it wishes. Moreover, when it wants to preserve the illusion of continuity, the Court can make new law by gradually expanding or contracting existing rules so that the change is detectable only by lawyers. Thus, the Taft Court was able to restrict government's power to regulate prices simply by narrowing the definition of "businesses affected with a public interest."

Even the famous constitutional revolution of 1937 left the old rational relation test in place, simply substituting a deferential approach for the conservative-activist approach that had characterized the pre-1937 Court.

In this regard, it is interesting to note that many of the major doctrines of Supreme Court law are doubled-edged and can be used, in different contexts, by conservatives and liberals alike to achieve their goals. During the first century and a half of Supreme Court history, for example, judicial activism was a tactic normally used to further conservative ends, and judicial restraint was the rallying cry of the liberals. In contrast, the post-1937 liberals took over the activist approach, and the conservatives increasingly adopted the Holmesian doctrine of judicial restraint. In short, once a legal doctrine has been developed, it takes on a life of its own and may be put to uses unforeseen by and even opposite to the desires of the original creators.

Similarly, history suggests that some major ideological issues are largely red herrings which conceal rather than reveal the realities that underlie the Court's decisions. Charles Warren, the leading Supreme Court historian, contended that the States' rights doctrine has been used in this manner.[1] According to Warren, concrete cases are normally decided on the basis of whose ox is being gored, and States' rights arguments are invoked primarily to provide abstract rationalizations for the results. Thus, the Jeffersonians invoked States' rights to prevent the federal government from favoring the rich, but the four horsemen used the same theory to curtail federal efforts to help the poor. In fact, Supreme Court history teaches that the verbiage in many Court opinions is merely a screen, and that attentive students should look behind the words to the economic effects that actually explain the outcome.

Whither the Court now? All available signals suggest that, in the short run, the Court is headed still further to the right. The strongest bloc on the present Court—the five horsepersons, Rehnquist, Scalia, Kennedy, O'Connor, and White—have full control and need not even consider the views of the moderate-liberal opposition. Moreover, if

---

1. 1 Warren, *The Supreme Court*, 388: "[T]hroughout American history, devotion to State-Rights and opposition to the jurisdiction of the Federal Government, whether in the South or the North, has been based, not so much on dogmatic political theories or beliefs, as upon the particular economic, political or social legislation which the decision happened to sustain or overthrow. No State and no section of the Union has found any difficulty in adopting or opposing the State-Rights theory, whenever its interests lay that way."

Marshall, the last survivor of the once dominant liberal-activist wing, cannot outlast the Bush presidency, we may soon have a Court without a liberal wing. In short, the Court's third conservative era may still have a long way to go before the pendulum begins to swing back in the other direction.

As a result, restraint and moderation are needed on the part of the conservative leaders who now dominate the executive branch. Consider the following likely scenario. What if the Court's most liberal members, Marshall, and Blackmun, die or retire soon? This is very possible since they are both 82. If President Bush uses the appointments to placate conservative Republicans, we are likely to have two more hard-line conservatives join the already dominant Rehnquist wing. The "Bush Court," then, would look like this:

TABLE 28
Alignment of Justices, 1995

Left	Center	Right
	Stevens	Rehnquist
		Scalia
		Kennedy
		Souter
		O'Connor
		White
		Doe
		Roe

Would this be good for the country? The answer seems to be plainly no. As Brandeis pointed out so many times, the greatest domestic danger to American society is the failure of free enterprise capitalism to make the adjustments needed to cure real injustice and prevent the emergence of widespread, violent dissatisfaction. Since 1968, the nation has increasingly turned its back on the poor. The tax revolt; the dismantling of the New Deal and the Great Society; deregulation; the policy of increased welfare for the military-industrial complex and across-the-board cuts for the poor—all these will lead to a day of reckoning unless the main organs of government are perceived as fair and representative of the poor as well as the rich.

The time seems to be at hand for the Supreme Court to moderate its course and eschew the right-wing pattern that has increasingly characterized its third conservative era. Ironically, however, the main attacks on the Court are still coming from the right, and the Justices themselves are calling for less rather than more liberal activism. The Nixon-Reagan agenda has worked too well, and it may soon be necessary to rechisel the motto on the Court's pediment to read, "Justice for the Rich." Let us hope sound judgment prevails and the Court once again resumes the balanced position needed to insure equal justice under law.

It is too early to tell whether the Warren Court's assumption of the role of special protector of the poor and disenfranchised was a passing aberration or a harbinger of things to come. History certainly suggests that the Supreme Court has a greater tendency toward economic conservatism than economic liberalism. Nevertheless, it is also true that the constitutional revolution of 1937 put an apparent end to the Court's career as constitutional censor of economic reform legislation and created a need for the Court to be reborn in a new image. Thus, the historical data from the pre-1937 period may be less relevant to the future of the Court than the legal developments that emerged in the 1940's and 1960's.

If this is so, the future may show the Burger and Rehnquist Courts to be historical anachronisms and the Warren Court to be the bellwether of a new era in which the Supreme Court throws off its traditional image and begins to make an active contribution to democratic government by protecting and advancing the interests of those groups who have traditionally been powerless and disenfranchised.

In the short run, however, the Justices clearly favor the rich, and the best strategy for advocates of the poor is to stay out of the Supreme Court as much as possible and to focus their economic reform efforts in the federal and State legislatures.

Index

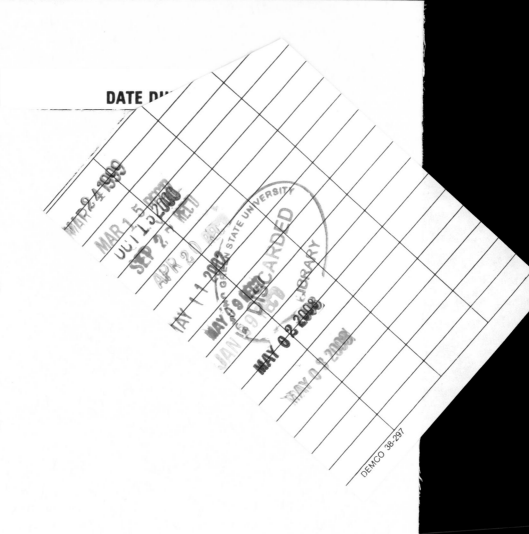